TEACHER'S PET PUBLICATIONS

LITPLAN TEACHER PACK
for
Travels with Charley
based on the book by
John Steinbeck

Written by
Mary B. Collins

© 2005 Teacher's Pet Publications
All Rights Reserved

This **LitPlan** for
Travels With Charley
has been brought to you by Teacher's Pet Publications, Inc.

Copyright Teacher's Pet Publications 2005
11504 Hammock Point
Berlin MD 21811

Only the student materials in this unit plan (such as worksheets, study questions, and tests) may be reproduced multiple times for use in the purchaser's classroom.

For any additional copyright questions,
contact Teacher's Pet Publications.

www.teacherspetpublications.com

TABLE OF CONTENTS - *Travels With Charley*

Introduction	5
Unit Objectives	7
Reading Assignment Sheet	8
Unit Outline	9
Study Questions (Short Answer)	13
Quiz/Study Questions (Multiple Choice)	21
Pre-reading Vocabulary Worksheets	39
Lesson One (Introductory Lesson)	57
Nonfiction Assignment Sheet	60
Oral Reading Evaluation Form	66
Writing Assignment 1	64
Writing Assignment 2	71
Writing Assignment 3	75
Writing Evaluation Form	72
Vocabulary Review Activities	81
Extra Writing Assignments/Discussion ?s	78
Unit Review Activities	82
Unit Tests	93
Unit Resource Materials	125
Vocabulary Resource Materials	149

A FEW NOTES ABOUT THE AUTHOR
JOHN STEINBECK

STEINBECK, John (1902-68). Winner of the 1962 Nobel prize for literature, the American author John Steinbeck is best remembered for his novel 'The Grapes of Wrath'. Steinbeck's story of a family of farm workers migrating from Oklahoma to California describes the hopelessness of the Great Depression era.

John Ernst Steinbeck was born on Feb. 27, 1902, in Salinas, Calif. He took classes at Stanford University for several years but left without a degree. He worked as a laborer to support himself while he wrote. Steinbeck's first novel was published in 1929, but it was not until the publication of 'Tortilla Flat' in 1935 that he attained critical and popular acclaim.

He followed this success with 'In Dubious Battle' (1936) and 'Of Mice and Men' (1937). 'The Grapes of Wrath' (1939) earned for Steinbeck a Pulitzer prize. In these works Steinbeck's proletarian themes are expressed through his portrayal of the inarticulate, dispossessed laborers who populate his American landscape. Both 'Of Mice and Men' and 'The Grapes of Wrath' were made into motion pictures.

In 1943 Steinbeck traveled to North Africa and Italy as a war correspondent. Some of his later works include 'Cannery Row' (1945), 'The Pearl' (1947), 'East of Eden' (1952), 'The Winter of Our Discontent' (1961), and 'Travels with Charley' (1962). He also wrote several motion-picture scripts, including adaptations of two of his shorter works-'The Pearl' and 'The Red Pony'. Steinbeck died in New York City on Dec. 20, 1968.

---- Courtesy of Compton's Learning Company

INTRODUCTION

This LitPlan has been designed to develop students' reading, writing, thinking, and language skills through exercises and activities related to *Travels With Charley*. It includes 19 lessons, supported by extra resource materials. There is an extra project at the end which would add 8 lessons.

The **introductory lesson** introduces students to the idea of traveling in America. Following the introductory activity, students are given a transition to explain how the activity relates to the book they are about to read. Following the transition, students are given the materials they will be using during the unit. At the end of the lesson, students begin the pre-reading work for the first reading assignment.

The **reading assignments** are approximately thirty pages each; some are a little shorter while others are a little longer. Students have approximately 15 minutes of pre-reading work to do prior to each reading assignment. This pre-reading work involves reviewing the study questions for the assignment and doing some vocabulary work for 8 to 10 vocabulary words they will encounter in their reading.

The **study guide questions** are fact-based questions; students can find the answers to these questions right in the text. These questions come in two formats: short answer or multiple choice. The best use of these materials is probably to use the short answer version of the questions as study guides for students (since answers will be more complete), and to use the multiple choice version for occasional quizzes.

The **vocabulary work** is intended to enrich students' vocabularies as well as to aid in the students' understanding of the book. Prior to each reading assignment, students will complete a two-part worksheet for approximately 8 to 10 vocabulary words in the upcoming reading assignment. Part I focuses on students' use of general knowledge and contextual clues by giving the sentence in which the word appears in the text. Students are then to write down what they think the words mean based on the words' usage. Part II nails down the definitions of the words by giving students dictionary definitions of the words and having students match the words to the correct definitions based on the words' contextual usage. Students should then have an understanding of the words when they meet them in the text.

After each reading assignment, students will go back and formulate answers for the study guide questions. Discussion of these questions serves as a **review** of the most important events and ideas presented in the reading assignments.

After students complete reading the work, there is a **vocabulary review** lesson which pulls together all of the fragmented vocabulary lists for the reading assignments and gives students a review of all of the words they have studied.

A lesson is devoted to the **extra discussion questions/writing assignments**. These questions focus on interpretation, critical analysis and personal response, employing a variety of thinking skills and adding to the students' understanding of the novel.

There is a **group project** in this unit. Students choose a city in America, research a variety of aspects about that city, prepare a written report for grading, and give an oral report to the class. These reports can easily be compiled into a published booklet for all the students to have.

There are three **writing assignments** in this unit, each with the purpose of informing, persuading, or having students be creative or express personal opinions. In the first writing assignment, students write to inform; it is their written report about their cities. The second writing assignment is creative: students create an episode to add to *Travels With Charley*. The third writing assignment is both creative and persuasive. Students write an episode to add to the book, but this time the episode has to be Steinbeck's encounter with a Cheerleader, persuading her to change her attitudes.

There is a **nonfiction reading assignment**. Students must read nonfiction articles, books, etc. to gather information about their themes in our world today.

The **review lesson** pulls together all of the aspects of the unit. The teacher is given four or five choices of activities or games to use which all serve the same basic function of reviewing all of the information presented in the unit.

The **unit test** comes in two formats: multiple choice or short answer. As a convenience, two different tests for each format have been included. There is also an advanced short answer unit test for advanced students.

There are additional **support materials** included with this unit. The **Unit Resource Materials** section includes suggestions for an in-class library, crossword and word search puzzles related to the novel, and extra worksheets. There is a list of **bulletin board ideas** which gives the teacher suggestions for bulletin boards to go along with this unit. In addition, there is a list of **extra class activities** the teacher could choose from to enhance the unit or as a substitution for an exercise the teacher might feel is inappropriate for his/her class. **Answer keys** are located directly after the **reproducible student materials** throughout the unit. The **Vocabulary Resource Materials** section includes similar worksheets and games to reinforce the vocabulary words.

The **level** of this unit can be varied depending upon the criteria on which the individual assignments are graded, the teacher's expectations of his/her students in class discussions, and the formats chosen for the study guides, quizzes and test. If teachers have other ideas/activities they wish to use, they can usually easily be inserted prior to the review lesson.

The student materials may be reproduced for use in the teacher's classroom without infringement of copyrights. No other portion of this unit may be reproduced without the written consent of Teacher's Pet Publications, Inc.

UNIT OBJECTIVES

1. Students will become better acquainted with the United States.

2. Students will discuss many issues facing cities and towns today.

3. Students will practice reading out loud and silently.

4. Students will answer questions to demonstrate their knowledge and understanding of the main events and characters in *Travels With Charley*, as they relate to the author's theme development.

5. Students will research and share information about major U. S. cities.

6. The writing assignments are designed for several purposes:
    a. To check and increase students reading comprehension
    b. To make students think about the ideas presented in the novel
    c. To encourage logical thinking
    d. To provide the opportunity for students to practice good grammar and improve their use of the language
    e. To encourage students' creativity
    f. To practice writing practical letters of request

7. Students will participate in group activities to improve their personal interaction skills.

8. Students will study vocabulary from the book to improve their own vocabularies.

9. Students will practice their public speaking skills.

READING ASSIGNMENTS *Travels With Charley*

As you know, *Travels With Charley* is divided into four main parts. However, within each part there are divisions. Because there are different editions in use, the page numbers for the reading assignments change. We have gone through the text and marked each division in the story as a "chapter" and given it a number (in chronological order). We thought this would be the easiest way to make the reading assignments clear to you. As an additional help, we have also written in the beginning sentence or phrase from each "chapter."

Assignment #	"Chapters"	Begins with the phrase or sentence...
1	1 - 4	"When I was very young . . ."
2	5 - 6	"Preparation for the Winter in New England is drastic."
3	7 - 8	"Niagara Falls is very nice."
4	9 - 12	"Chicago was a break in my journey . . ."
5	13 - 15	"The next passage in my journey is a love affair."
6	16 - 21	"Now, there is not any question that Charley was rapidly becoming a tree expert."
7	22 - 26	"When I started this narrative . . . "

Date Assigned	Assignment	Completion Date
	1	
	2	
	3	
	4	
	5	
	6	
	7	

UNIT OUTLINE *Travels With Charley*

1 Introduction Travelogue	2 City Assign. Writing 1	3 PVR 1-4	4 Study ??s 1-4 Read 5-6	5 Study ?? 5-6 PVR 7-8
6 Library Day	7 PVR 9-12	8 Study ??s 9-15 Assign 16-21	9 Read 22-26	10 Writing 2 Assign ??s
11 Study ??s 16-26 Begin City Presentations	12 City Presentations	13 Extra Discussion Questions	14 Review	15 Test
16 Travel Agent Assign Project	17 Project Work	18 Project Work	19 Project Work	20 Project Work
21 Writing Assignment	22 Presentations	23 Presentations	24 Presentations	

STUDY GUIDE QUESTIONS

SHORT ANSWER STUDY GUIDE QUESTIONS - *Travels With Charley*

Reading Assignment #1 ("Chapters" 1-4)
  1. Describe the type of vehicle Steinbeck required for his journey.
  2. Where did Steinbeck begin his journey?
  3. Identify Rocinante.
  4. Describe Steinbeck's traveling companion.
  5. Identify Fayre Eleyne.
  6. For whom was the boat named?
  7. What did Steinbeck see in the eyes of many of the people he met during his journey?
  8. In what ways did American cities and towns look the same?
  9. Where did Steinbeck like to observe people?

Reading Assignment #2 ("Chapters" 5 & 6)
  1. Describe Steinbeck's method for washing his clothes during his trip.
  2. What was Steinbeck's impression of Deer Isle?
  3. How did Steinbeck protect Charley in Maine during hunting season?
  4. Why did Steinbeck head for Aroostook County, Maine?
  5. What does vacilando mean?
  6. From where were the Maine migrant farmers?
  7. In which state are the White Mountains?
  8. What was different about the Sunday sermon given in the church in Vermont?

Reading Assignment #3 ("Chapters" 7 & 8)
  1. Why didn't Steinbeck cross the Canadian border?
  2. What was Steinbeck's opinion of super-highways?
  3. What clannish group of people who speak a specialized language did Steinbeck discover on the super-highways?
  4. Why was coffee considered the great get-together symbol?
  5. Why did Steinbeck consider mobile homes to be a revolution in living?
  6. What questions did Steinbeck have about Americans and roots?
  7. To what was Charley allergic?
  8. What difference in people did Steinbeck notice as he crossed the Ohio line?
  9. What were Steinbeck's observations about regional speech?
10. Who came to visit Steinbeck in Chicago?
11. How did Steinbeck find the Ambassador East hotel?
12. Identify Lonesome Harry.

Travels With Charley Study Questions

Reading Assignment #4 ("Chapters" 9 - 12)
  1. How was Charley torn three ways?
  2. What are the Wisconsin Dells?
  3. What are the Twin Cities?
  4. What are the W.P.A. Guides to the States?
  5. Where in the country did Steinbeck find the east-west middle of the country?
  6. Where in the country did Steinbeck believe the east-west middle should be?
  7. What area of the country seemed like the work of an evil child?

Reading Assignment #5 ("Chapters" 13 - 15)
  1. What state did Steinbeck fall in love with and consider to be a great splash of grandeur?
  2. What did Steinbeck learn about Charley at Yellowstone?
  3. What did Steinbeck tell Robbie's father about hairdressers?
  4. Describe Charley's ailment and Steinbeck's solution to the problem.

Reading Assignment #6 ("Chapters" 16 - 21)
  1. What tree causes wonder and respect in men?
  2. Redwoods were once located in England, Europe and America. What happened to them?
  3. Where was Steinbeck born?
  4. Why did Steinbeck go to Monterey?
  5. On what issue did Steinbeck and his sisters argue constantly?
  6. For whom was Charley named?
  7. While crossing the Mojave Desert, how did Steinbeck and Charley cool off?
  8. At first, Steinbeck considered killing the coyotes. What did he finally do?
  9. What factor found in all living things was especially present in the desert?

Reading Assignment #7 ("Chapters" 22 - 26)
  1. Which state is the only state that came into the Union in a treaty?
  2. Why did Texas seek freedom from Mexico?
  3. What are the reasons Steinbeck felt that he could not be objective about Texas?
  4. Why was Charley left in Amarillo?
  5. Why did Steinbeck dread traveling to the South?
  6. Who were the Coopers?
  7. Why did Steinbeck choose to go to New Orleans?
  8. Who were the Cheerleaders?
  9. Besides the black student, who else did the Cheerleaders verbally assault?
10. What did the southerners think about northerners?
11. Where during his trip did Steinbeck's journey end before he returned home?
12. Why couldn't Rocinante go through the Holland Tunnel?
13. What was the final event of Steinbeck's journey?

STUDY GUIDE QUESTIONS ANSWER KEY *Travels With Charley*

Reading Assignment #1 ("Chapters" 1-4)
1. Describe the type of vehicle Steinbeck required for his journey.
    He needed a four-wheel drive, 3/4 ton pick-up truck with a camper top.

2. Where did Steinbeck begin his journey?
    He started at Sag Harbor, New York.

3. Identify Rocinante.
    Rocinante was the name Steinbeck gave his truck.

4. Describe Steinbeck's traveling companion.
    He was a french poodle named Charley.

5. Identify Fayre Eleyne.
    Fayre Eleyne was the name of Steinbeck's boat.

6. For whom was the boat named?
    The boat was named for Steinbeck's wife.

7. What did Steinbeck see in the eyes of many of the people he met during his journey?
    He saw a look of longing. People wished to be able to do what he was doing.

8. In what ways did American cities and towns look the same?
    All were ringed with trash, surrounded by rusting and wrecked vehicles, and were smothered by rubbish.

9. Where did Steinbeck like to observe people?
    He went to bars, churches and roadside restaurants. He also listened to the morning radio.

Reading Assignment #2 ("Chapters" 5 & 6)
1. Describe Steinbeck's method for washing his clothes during his trip.
    He placed the clothes, soap and water into a garbage bucket tied to the closet pole in the back of his truck. The truck's movement juggled the contents for the entire driving day. He rinsed the clothes at the end of the day, and dried them the next day on a line in the truck.

2. What was Steinbeck's impression of Deer Isle?
    He said that it is like Avalon; it disappears when you are not there.

3. How did Steinbeck protect Charley in Maine during hunting season?
>He wrapped Charley's tail in red Kleenex so he would not be mistaken for a deer.

4. Why did Steinbeck head for Aroostook County, Maine?
>He wanted to see the potato crops.

5. What does vacilando mean?
>It describes the act of going somewhere with a direction in mind but not caring whether or not you get there.

6. From where were the Maine migrant farmers?
>They were French Canadians called Canucks.

7. In which state are the White Mountains?
>They are in Maine.

8. What was different about the Sunday sermon given in the church in Vermont?
>It was an old-fashioned "fire and brimstone" sermon.

Reading Assignment #3 ("Chapters" 7 & 8)

1. Why didn't Steinbeck cross the Canadian border?
>He didn't have a rabies vaccination certificate for Charley. The U.S. would not let him re-enter the country without that certificate.

2. What was Steinbeck's opinion of super-highways?
>He thought that they were wonderful for moving goods, but that they were not very good for people who were interested in seeing the countryside of America.

3. What clannish group of people who speak a specialized language did Steinbeck discover on the super-highways?
>He discovered long-distance truckers.

4. Why was coffee considered the great get-together symbol?
>Having a cup of coffee provided the chance to rest and to have a change from the continuous stretch of highway.

5. Why did Steinbeck consider mobile homes to be a revolution in living?
>He thought they were comfortable, compact, easy to keep clean, and easy to heat.

6. What questions did Steinbeck have about Americans and roots?
   Are Americans restless and never satisfied? Is the need or urge to be somewhere else greater than the need for roots?

7. To what was Charley allergic?
   He was allergic to insecticides.

8. What difference in people did Steinbeck notice as he crossed the Ohio line?
   The people became open and out-going.

9. What were Steinbeck's observations about regional speech?
   He thought that regional speech was perhaps disappearing because people were listening to radio and television voices so much.

10. Who came to visit Steinbeck in Chicago?
    His wife came.

11. How did Steinbeck find the Ambassador East hotel?
    He hired a taxi to lead the way.

12. Identify Lonesome Harry.
    He was the former occupant of Steinbeck's hotel room at the Ambassador East.

Reading Assignment #4 ("Chapters" 9 - 12)

1. How was Charley torn three ways?
   He had anger towards Steinbeck for leaving him, he was happy to see Rocinante, and he had a certain pride in his appearance.

2. What are the Wisconsin Dells?
   The Wisconsin Dells are formations in the countryside sculptured by the ice in the Ice Age.

3. What are the Twin Cities?
   The Twin Cities are Minneapolis and St. Paul.

4. What are the W.P.A. Guides to the States?
   They are a complete set of books which give a comprehensive account of the geography, history and economy of the U.S.A.

5. Where in the country did Steinbeck find the east-west middle of the country?
   He found the middle in Fargo, North Dakota.

6. Where in the country did Steinbeck believe the east-west middle should be?
    He thought it should be at the Missouri River at Bismarck, North Dakota.

7. What area of the country seemed like the work of an evil child?
    The Bad Lands did.

Reading Assignment #5 ("Chapters" 13 - 15)
1. What state did Steinbeck fall in love with and consider to be a great splash of grandeur?
    Montana

2. What did Steinbeck learn about Charley at Yellowstone?
    He found out that Charley was not as peace-loving and cowardly as he had believed. Charley wanted to fight the bears!

3. What did Steinbeck tell Robbie's father about hairdressers?
    He told him that women confided in their hairdressers and that gave the hairdressers a lot of power.

4. Describe Charley's ailment and Steinbeck's solution to the problem.
    Charley had bladder problems and could not urinate. Steinbeck gave him sleeping pills to make him relax so he could rid himself of fluid.

Reading Assignment #6 ("Chapters" 16 - 21)
1. What tree causes wonder and respect in men?
    The giant redwood trees do.

2. Redwoods were once located in England, Europe and America. What happened to them?
    They were wiped out by the moving glaciers.

3. Where was Steinbeck born?
    He was born in Salinas, California.

4. Why did Steinbeck go to Monterey?
    He wanted to cast his absentee ballot.

5. On what issue did Steinbeck and his sisters argue constantly?
    They argued about politics.

6. For whom was Charley named?
    He was named for Steinbeck's Uncle Charley.

7. While crossing the Mojave Desert, how did Steinbeck and Charley cool off?
>   They poured water over themselves. (The air was so dry that the water's evaporating made them feel cool.)

8. At first, Steinbeck considered killing the coyotes. What did he finally do?
>   He opened two cans of dog food and left them for the coyotes.

9. What factor found in all living things was especially present in the desert?
>   The will and need to survive was especially strong in the desert life.

Reading Assignment #7 ("Chapters" 22 - 26)

1. Which state is the only state that came into the Union in a treaty?
>   Texas is the only one.

2. Why did Texas seek freedom from Mexico?
>   The Texans didn't want to pay taxes. Also, Mexico had abolished slavery and the Texans did not want to free their slaves.

3. What are the reasons Steinbeck felt that he could not be objective about Texas?
>   He knew the countryside and had friends and relations in that state.

4. Why was Charley left in Amarillo?
>   He was recovering from another illness.

5. Why did Steinbeck dread traveling to the South?
>   He knew he would see pain, fear, bewilderment and confusion caused by desegregation.

6. Who were the Coopers?
>   They were the only black family in Salinas, the only black family Steinbeck had known during his childhood.

7. Why did Steinbeck choose to go to New Orleans?
>   He wanted to witness the school desegregation.

8. Who were the Cheerleaders?
>   They were a group of white women who would gather at the school to scream at the black students.

9. Besides the black student, who else did the Cheerleaders verbally assault?
>They also verbally assaulted the white man who brought his white child to school.

10. What did the southerners think about northerners?
>They thought that the northerners came to the south to cause trouble and to stir things up.

11. Where during his trip did Steinbeck's journey end before he returned home?
>His trip was really finished at Abingdon, Virginia. By the time he got there, he had had enough time on the road, was tired, overloaded with input, and ready to put up his feet in his own home.

12. Why couldn't Rocinante go through the Holland Tunnel?
>The truck carried butane tanks which were not allowed in the tunnel.

13. What was the final event of Steinbeck's journey?
>He got lost in his own hometown.

STUDY GUIDE/QUIZ QUESTIONS - *Travels With Charley*
Multiple Choice Format

Chapters 1-4

1. Describe the type of vehicle Steinbeck required for his journey.
	A. He needed a 6 cylinder mini-van with a tow bar.
	B. He needed a station wagon with air conditioning.
	C. He needed a motorcycle with a side car.
	D. He needed a four-wheel drive, 3/4 ton pick-up truck with a camper top.

2. Where did Steinbeck begin his journey?
	A. He started at Salinas, California.
	B. He started at Sag Harbor, New York.
	C. He started at Deerfield, Massachusetts.
	D. He started at Chicago, Illinois.

3. What did Steinbeck name his truck?
	A. Rocinante
	B. Betelguese
	C. Road Warrior
	D. Gulliver

4. Who was Charley?
	A. He was a Siamese cat.
	B. He was a french poodle.
	C. He was Steinbeck son.
	D. He was Steinbeck brother.

5. _____ was the name of Steinbeck's boat.
	A. Lady Donna
	B. Pearlie B
	C. Fayre Eleyne
	D. Neptuna

6. For whom was the boat named?
	A. The boat was named for Steinbeck mother.
	B. The boat was named for Steinbeck sister.
	C. The boat was named for Steinbeck daughter.
	D. The boat was named for Steinbeck's wife.

Travels With Charley Mutiple Choice Quiz Questions Chapters 1-4 Continued

7. True or False: Steinbeck saw a look of longing in the eyes of many of the people he met during his journey. People wished to be able to do what he was doing.
    A. True
    B. False

8. In what ways did American cities and towns look the same?
    A. They all had good public transportation systems, tall buildings downtown, and large airports.
    B. All were ringed with trash, surrounded by rusting and wrecked vehicles, and were smothered by rubbish.
    C. They all had modern highways, shopping malls, and pollution.
    D. They all had traffic jams, suburbs, and beautiful parks.

9. Where did Steinbeck like to observe people?
    A. He went to schools, bookstores, and concert halls.
    B. He went to libraries, department stores, and hospitals.
    C. He went to grocery stores, parks, and bus stations.
    D. He went to bars, churches and roadside restaurants.

10. What else did Steinbeck do to observe people?
    A. He sat around at airports.
    B. He picked up hitchhikers.
    C. He also listened to the morning radio.
    D. He read local newspapers.

Travels With Charley Mutiple Choice Quiz Questions Chapters 5-6

Chapters 5 & 6
1. What was Steinbeck doing? He placed the items into a garbage bucket tied to the closet pole in the back of his truck. The truck's movement juggled the contents for the entire driving day.
   A. He was washing his clothes.
   B. He was making ice cream.
   C. He was polishing rocks.
   D. He was making compost.

2. Steinbeck said that it is like Avalon; it disappears when you are not there. What place is this?
   A. Cape Cod
   B. Sanibel Island
   C. Deer Isle
   D. Catalina

3. How did Steinbeck protect Charley in Maine during hunting season?
   A. He wrapped Charley's tail in red kleenex so he would not be mistaken for a deer.
   B. He locked Charley in the truck at all times.
   C. He put Charley in a kennel.
   D. He put a bell around Charley neck so the hunters could hear him coming.

4. Why did Steinbeck head for Aroostook County, Maine?
   A. He wanted to visit a friend there.
   B. He wanted to see the potato crops.
   C. He wanted to go to an art exhibit.
   D. He was doing a personal appearance at a library.

5. What word means he act of going somewhere with a direction in mind but not caring whether or not you get there
   A. migrating
   B. vacilado
   C. sashay
   D. promenade

6. From where were the Maine migrant farmers?
   A. They were French Canadians called Canucks.
   B. They were Mexicans called Wetbacks.
   C. They were Puerto Ricans called Muchachos.
   D. They were Russians called Babushkas.

Travels With Charley Mutiple Choice Quiz Questions Chapters 5-6 Continued

7. In which state are the White Mountains?
    A. They are in New Hampshire.
    B. They are in Maine.
    C. They are in Vermont.
    D. They are in Massachusetts.

8. True or False: The Sunday sermon given in the church in Vermont was an old-fashioned "fire and brimstone" sermon.
    A. True
    B. False

Travels With Charley Mutiple Choice Quiz Questions Chapters 7-8

<u>Chapters 7 & 8</u>

1. True or False: Steinbeck didn cross the Canadian border because he had traffic ticket on his record. Canada would not let him in.
    A. True
    B. False

2. What was Steinbeck talking about? He thought that they were wonderful for moving goods, but that they were not very good for people who were interested in seeing the countryside of America.
    A. moving vans
    B. trains
    C. super-highways
    D. airplanes

3. What clannish group of people who speak a specialized language did Steinbeck discover on the super-highways?
    A. state troopers
    B. long-distance truckers
    C. bus drivers
    D. gas station attendants

4. _____ was considered the great get-together symbol?
    A. waving hello to someone
    B. treating a stranger to lunch
    C. talking on the telephone
    D. having a cup of coffee

5. What is Steinbeck taking about? He thought they were a revolution in living. He thought they were comfortable, compact, easy to keep clean, and easy to heat.
    A. mobile homes
    B. minivans
    C. passenger trains
    D. commuter airplanes

Travels With Charley Mutiple Choice Quiz Questions Chapters 7-8 Continued

6. What questions did Steinbeck have about Americans?
    A. Are Americans patriotic and content?
    B. Are Americans intelligent and rich?
    C. Are Americans selfish and destructive?
    D. Are Americans restless and never satisfied?

7. Finish Steinbeck question: Is the need or urge to be somewhere else greater than the need for _____?
    A. happiness
    B. roots
    C. wealth
    D. good health

8. To what was Charley allergic?
    A. He was allergic to insecticides.
    B. He was allergic to nuts.
    C. He was allergic to soap.
    D. He was allergic to cats.

9. True or False: Steinbeck noticed that people became closed and unfriendly as he crossed the Ohio line.
    A. True
    B. False

10. Steinbeck thought that _____ was perhaps disappearing because people were listening to radio and television voices so much.
    A. good grammar
    B. the art of public speaking
    C. regional speech
    D. conversation between friends

11. Who came to visit Steinbeck in Chicago?
    A. His wife did.
    B. His publisher did.
    C. His son did.
    D. His parents did.

Travels With Charley Mutiple Choice Quiz Questions Chapters 7-8 Continued

12. How did Steinbeck find the Ambassador East hotel?
    A. He called the hotel and had someone come to meet him.
    B. He took a bus there.
    C. He used online directions.
    D. He hired a taxi to lead the way.

13. _____ was the former occupant of Steinbeck's hotel room at the Ambassador East.
    A. Wandering Eddie
    B. Lonesome Harry
    C. Uncle Sam
    D. Duke Dan

Travels With Charley Mutiple Choice Quiz Questions Chapters 9-12

Chapters 9 - 12
1. Charley had anger towards Steinbeck for leaving him, he was happy to see Rocinante, and he had _____
    A. a certain pride in his appearance
    B. a desire to get back on the road
    C. a need to be loved
    D. motivation to show off his new training

2. The _____ are formations in the countryside sculptured by the ice in the Ice Age.
    A. Moraine Mountains
    B. Cambrian Cliffs
    C. Wisconsin Dells
    D. Kettles of Madison

3. What are the Twin Cities?
    A. Kansas City, Kansas and Kansas Ciaty, Missosuri
    B. Minneapolis and St. Paul, Minnesota
    C. Chicago, Illinois and Milwaukee, Wisconsin
    D. Duluth and Sioux Falls, Idaho

4. The _____ are a complete set of books which give a comprehensive account of the geography, history and economy of the U.S.A.
    A. *U. S. State Reports*
    B. *Highway How-To*
    C. *Motor Club Travel Journals*
    D. *W.P.A. Guides to the States*

5. Where in the country did Steinbeck find the east-west middle of the country?
    A. Fargo, North Dakota
    B. Detroit, Michigan
    C. Salt Lake City, Utah
    D. Bismark, South Dakota

6. Where in the country did Steinbeck believe the east-west middle should be?
    A. at the Continental Divide in Colorado
    B. at the Grand Canyon
    C. at the Missouri River at Bismarck, North Dakota
    D. at the Mississippi River in St. Louis, Missouri

Travels With Charley Mutiple Choice Quiz Questions Chapters 9-12 Continued

7. What area of the country seemed like the work of an evil child?
    A. Death Valley
    B. the Petrified Forest
    C. White Sands
    D. the Bad Lands

Travels With Charley Mutiple Choice Quiz Questions Chapters 13-15

Chapters 13 - 15
1. What state did Steinbeck fall in love with and consider to be a great splash of grandeur?
   A. Idaho
   B. Utah
   C. Montana
   D. Oregon

2. What did Charley want to do at Yellowstone?
   A. Charley wanted to swim in the water of Old Faithful.
   B. Charley wanted to play with the children he met.
   C. Charley wanted to fight the bears!
   D. Charley wanted to chase squirrels.

3. Steinbeck told Robbie's father that women confided in their _____ and that gave those people a lot of power.
   A. ministers
   B. hairdressers
   C. appliance repairmen
   D. husbands

4. Describe Charley's ailment.
   A. Charley had bladder problems and could not urinate.
   B. Charley had a splinter in his foot and could not walk.
   C. Charely had stomach problems and could not eat.
   D. Charley had motion sickness and couldn ride in the truck.

5. What was Steinbeck's solution to the problem?
   A. Steinbeck took him to a vet to get the splinter removed.
   B. Steinbeck gave him crackers and ginger ale to calm his stomach.
   C. Steinbeck put motion sickness bands on Charley
   D. Steinbeck gave him sleeping pills to make him relax so he could rid himself of fluid.

Travels With Charley Mutiple Choice Quiz Questions Chapters 16-21

Chapters 16 - 21
1. What tree causes wonder and respect in men?
	A. The live oak tree.
	B. The bonsai tree.
	C. The palm tree.
	D. The giant redwood tree.

2. These trees were once located in England, Europe and America. What happened to them?
	A. They were destroyed by gypsy moths.
	B. They were wiped out by the moving glaciers.
	C. They were cut down by loggers.
	D. They were burned in forest fires.

3. Where was Steinbeck born?
	A. He was born in Salinas, California.
	B. He was born in Santa Fe, New Mexico.
	C. He was born in New York City, New York.
	D. He was born in Milwaukee, Wisconsin.

4. Why did Steinbeck go to Monterey?
	A. He wanted to visit the aquarium.
	B. He wanted to cast his absentee ballot.
	C. He wanted to see an old friend.
	D. He wanted to go fishing.

5. On what issue did Steinbeck and his sisters argue constantly?
	A. They argued about family history.
	B. They argued about money.
	C. They argued about politics.
	D. They argued about food.

6. For whom was Charley named?
	A. He was named for Charlie Chaplin, the actor.
	B. He was named for a character in a book.
	C. He was named for Steinbeck's Uncle Charley.
	D. He was named for Steinbeck dead brother.

Travels With Charley Mutiple Choice Quiz Questions Chapters 16-21 Continued

7. While crossing the Mojave Desert, how did Steinbeck and Charley cool off?
    A. They drank cold sodas.
    B. They ate ice chips.
    C. They used the air conditioner in the truck.
    D. They poured water over themselves.

8. True or False: Steinbeck killed the coyotes.
    A. True
    B. False

9. What factor found in all living things was especially present in the desert?
    A. It was a spirit of cooperation.
    B. It was a fierce sense of competition.
    C. It was the will and need to survive.
    D. It was a relaxed attitude about life.

Travels With Charley Mutiple Choice Quiz Questions Chapters 22-26

Chapters 22 - 26

1. Which state is the only state that came into the Union in a treaty?
    A. Texas is the only one.
    B. Vermont is the only one.
    C. California is the only one.
    D. Virginia is the only one.

2. Texas wanted freedom from Mexico because the Texans didn't want to pay _____. Also, Mexico had _____ and the Texans did not want to do this.
    A. for the Mexican army; started a draft for the military
    B. taxes; abolished slavery
    C. to buy the land; mandatory education
    D. to support the Catholic church; a state religion

3. Why did Steinbeck feel that he could not be objective about Texas?
    A. He had had a bad experience there once.
    B. The only newspaper to give his books a bad review was in Texas.
    C. He had gone to school there and had fond memories.
    D. He knew the countryside and had friends and relations in that state.

4. Why was Charley left in Amarillo?
    A. He was recovering from another illness.
    B. It was too hot for him to travel.
    C. Steinbeck friend was lonely and asked for Charley to keep him company.
    D. There was not room for him in the truck, as Steinbeck was taking a human passenger.

5. Steinbeck dreaded traveling to the South because he knew he would see pain, fear, bewilderment and confusion caused by _____.
    A. poverty
    B. war
    C. desegregation
    D. religion

6. The Coopers were the only ____ family in Salinas, the only ones Steinbeck had known during his childhood.
    A. black
    B. Mexican
    C. Irish
    D. Mormon

Travels With Charley Mutiple Choice Quiz Questions Chapters 22-26 Continued

7. Steinbeck chose to go to _____ because he wanted to witness the school desegregation.
    A. Boston
    B. New Orleans
    C. Atlanta
    D. Selma

8. The _____ were a group of white women who would gather at the school to scream at the black students.
    A. Klanettes
    B. White Women for Segregation
    C. Hospitality Club
    D. Cheerleaders

9. True or False: Besides the black student, the group of white women beat up a white child who came to the school.
    A. True
    B. False

10. True or False: The southerners thought that the northerners came to the south to cause trouble and to stir things up.
    A. True
    B. False

11. Where during his trip did Steinbeck's journey end before he returned home?
    A. His trip was really finished at
    B. His trip was really finished at
    C. His trip was really finished at
    D. His trip was really finished at Abingdon, Virginia.

12. True or False: By the time he got to his last stop, Steinbeck was ready to start all over on another trip.
    A. True
    B. False

13. Rocinante could not go _____ because the truck carried butane tanks which were not allowed there.
    A. across the Brooklyn Bridge
    B. through the Holland Tunnel
    C. into downtown New York City
    D. on the Staten Island Ferry

Travels With Charley Mutiple Choice Quiz Questions Chapters 22-26 Continued

14. What was the final event of Steinbeck's journey?
    A. Someone stole the truck from his driveway.
    B. The town had a parade for him.
    C. He got lost in his own hometown.
    D. Charley died.

ANSWER KEY - MULTIPLE CHOICE STUDY/QUIZ QUESTIONS
Travels With Charley

	1-4	5-6	7-8	9-12	13-15	16-21	22-26
1	D	A	B	A	C	D	A
2	B	C	C	C	C	B	B
3	A	A	B	B	B	A	D
4	B	B	D	D	A	B	A
5	C	B	A	A	D	C	C
6	D	A	D	C		C	A
7	A	B	B	D		D	B
8	B	A	A			B	D
9	D		B			C	B
10	C		C				A
11			A				D
12			D				B
13			B				B
14							C

PREREADING VOCABULARY WORKSHEETS

VOCABULARY CHAPTERS 1-4 *Travels With Charley*

Part I: Using Prior Knowledge and Contextual Clues

Below are the sentences in which the vocabulary words appear in the text. Read the sentence. Use any clues you can find in the sentence combined with your prior knowledge, and write what you think the underlined words mean on the lines provided.

1. A journey is a person in itself; no two are alike. And all plans, safeguards, policing, and coercion are fruitless. We find after years of struggle that we do not take a trip; a trip takes us.

   _____

2. My plan was clear, concise, and reasonable, I think.

   _____

3. This being so, my trip demanded that I leave my name and my identity at home. I had to be peripatetic eyes and ears, a kind of moving gelatin plate.

   _____

4. It is well known that our roads are dangerous. And here I admit I had senseless qualms.

   _____

5. He stood apart shyly and looked at Rocinante; he peered in the door, even lay on the ground and studied the heavy-duty springs. He was a silent, ubiquitous small boy.

   _____

6. With a hurricane approaching we prepared to stand a siege.

   _____

7. As the day approached, my warm bed and comfortable house grew increasingly desirable and my dear wife incalculably precious.

   _____

8. I knew that ten or twelve thousand miles driving a truck, alone and unattended, over every kind of road, would be hard work, but to me it represented the antidote for the poison of the professional sick man.

   _____

Travels With Charley Vocabulary Worksheet Chapters 1-4 Continued

9. He looked at me with the contained amusement that is considered <u>taciturnity</u> by non-Yankees.

_____

10. Breakfast conversation is limited to a series of <u>laconic</u> grunts.

_____

11. She said the autumn never failed to amaze her; to <u>elate</u>. "It is a glory," she said, "and can't be remembered, so that it always comes as a surprise."

Part II: Determining the Meaning
   Match the vocabulary words to their dictionary definitions

   ___ 1. Coercion   A. Bad or uneasy feelings
   ___ 2. Concise   B. Not talkative
   ___ 3. Peripatetic   C. Raise the spirits of; make joyful
   ___ 4. Qualms   D. Expressing much in a few words
   ___ 5. Ubiquitous   E. Anything that relieves or counteracts an injurious effect
   ___ 6. Siege   F. Terse; concise; succinct
   ___ 7. Precious   G. The surrounding and blockading of a town or fortress by
                              an army trying to capture it.
   ___ 8. Antidote   H. Valuable
   ___ 9. Taciturn   I. Roaming; wandering
   ___ 10. Laconic   J. To force to think or act in a certain manner
   ___ 11. Elate   K. Seeming to be everywhere at one time

VOCABULARY CHAPTERS 5-6 *Travels With Charley*

Part I: Using Prior Knowledge and Contextual Clues

Below are the sentences in which the vocabulary words appear in the text. Read the sentence. Use any clues you can find in the sentence combined with your prior knowledge, and write what you think the underlined words mean on the lines provided.

1. My excuse is that in this era of planned <u>obsolescence</u>, when a thing breaks down I can usually find something in my collection to repair it--

_____

2. Strange how one person can saturate a room with <u>vitality</u>, with excitement.

_____

3. I <u>vaguely</u> remembered that I should be on U. S. Highway 1

_____

4,5. And he could never know that Charley's interest in him was purely <u>courteous</u>; if he did, he would be hurt in his <u>misanthropy</u>, for Charley has no interest in cats whatever, even for chasing purposes.

_____

_____

6. He isn't good company, he is not sympathetic, and he has little <u>aesthetic</u> value.

_____

7. George would have found his, or rather her, end in a bonfire, because if ever there was a familiar, an <u>envoy</u> of the devil, a consorter with evil spirits, George is it.

_____

8. As often as I could I chose the small wood roads, and they are not <u>conducive</u> to speed.

_____

9. I retrieve him so that he will not be a <u>nuisance</u> to my neighbors--

_____

Travels With Charley Vocabulary Worksheet Chapters 5-6 Continued

10. Then I strolled to the camp to relieve my neighbors of the inconvenience of my miserable <u>cur</u>.

_____

11. I am an <u>avid</u> reader of all signs

_____

12. Genealogists are worked to death winnowing the <u>debris</u> of ancestry for grains of greatness.

_____

Part II: Determining the Meaning
    Match the vocabulary words to their dictionary definitions

    ____ 1. Obsolescence   A. Eager
    ____ 2. Vitality   B. Polite
    ____ 3. Vaguely   C. Being replaced by something newer
    ____ 4. Courteous   D. Not clearly expressed or defined
    ____ 5. Misanthropy   E. Scattered remains of something broken
    ____ 6. Aesthetic   F. An inferior or undesirable dog
    ____ 7. Envoy   G. Energy; liveliness
    ____ 8. Conducive   H. Hatred of mankind
    ____ 9. Nuisance   I. Messenger
    ____ 10. Cur   J. Source of inconvenience or bother
    ____ 11. Avid   K. Pertaining to the sense of beauty
    ____ 12. Debris   L. Helping to bring about an event

VOCABULARY CHAPTERS 7-8 *Travels With Charley*

Part I: Using Prior Knowledge and Contextual Clues

Below are the sentences in which the vocabulary words appear in the text. Read the sentence. Use any clues you can find in the sentence combined with your prior knowledge, and write what you think the underlined words mean on the lines provided.

1. . . . nowhere is my natural <u>anarchism</u> more aroused than at national borders where patient and efficient public servants carry out their duties in matters on immigration and customs.

   _____

2. Maybe the greater the urge, the deeper and more ancient is the need, the will, the hunger to be somewhere else. Charley had no answer to my <u>premise</u>.

   _____

3. But it is true that we have exchanged <u>corpulence</u> for starvation, and either one will kill us.

   _____

4. All this came through in small, <u>oblique</u> spirts in his conversation.

   _____

5. I have no desire to latch onto a monster symbol of fate and prove my manhood in titanic <u>piscine</u> war.

   _____

6. . . . but when he found he was to be left and in Chicago, his ordinary <u>aplomb</u> broke down and he cried out in rage and despair.

   _____

7. Also, I am not shy about admitting that I am an <u>incorrigible</u> Peeping-Tom.

   _____

Travels With Charley Vocabulary Worksheet Chapters 7-8 Continued

Part II: Determining the Meaning
    Match the vocabulary words to their dictionary definitions

    ___ 1. Anarchism   A. Relating to fish
    ___ 2. Premise   B. Indirect or evasive in meaning or expression; not straightforward
    ___ 3. Corpulence   C. Can't be corrected or reformed
    ___ 4. Oblique   D. Theory that all governments are bad and should be abolished.
    ___ 5. Piscine   E. Poise; self-confidence; assurance
    ___ 6. Aplomb   F. Being fat
    ___ 7. Incorrigible   G. A statement on which an argument is based or from which a conclusion is drawn

VOCABULARY CHAPTERS 9-12 *Travels With Charley*

Part I: Using Prior Knowledge and Contextual Clues
Below are the sentences in which the vocabulary words appear in the text. Read the sentence. Use any clues you can find in the sentence combined with your prior knowledge, and write what you think the underlined words mean on the lines provided.

1, 2, 3. Clinging to the sides of the dreamlike waterways was the litter of our times, the motels, the hot-dog stands, the merchants of the cheap and mediocre and tawdry so loved by summer tourists, but these incrustations were closed and boarded against the winter and, even open, I doubt that the could dispel the enchantment of the Wisconsin Dells

_____

_____

_____

4. And suddenly I thought of that valley of the turkeys and wondered how I could have the gall to think turkeys stupid.

_____

5. . . . more depressed than any other group while maintaining their inalienable instinct for eating.

_____

6. Fargo to me is brother to the fabulous places of the earth, kin to those magically remote spots mentioned by Herodotus and Marco Polo and Mandeville.

_____

7. . . . and I believe that subtleties of feeling began to disappear until finally I was on a pleasure-pain basis.

_____

8. If this people has so atrophied its taste buds as to find tasteless food not only acceptable but desirable, what of the emotional life of the nation?

_____

9. . . . a vintage sedan pulling a short coupled trailer like a ox turtle lumbered down from the road and took a position on the water

_____

45

Travels With Charley Vocabulary Worksheet Chapters 9-12 Continued

10. I saw he was not young. . . . And his eyes, large warm brown irises set on whites that were turning yellow, <u>corroborated</u> this.

_____

Part II: Determining the Meaning
    Match the vocabulary words to their dictionary definitions

    ___ 1. Mediocre   A. Relatives
    ___ 2. Tawdry   B. Neither good or bad; average; ordinary; commonplace
    ___ 3. Dispel   C. Details; refinements
    ___ 4. Gall   D. Classic; characterized by enduring appeal
    ___ 5. Inalienable   E. Gaudy and cheap
    ___ 6. Kin   F. Nerve; impudence
    ___ 7. Subtleties   G. Attest to the truth or accuracy of something
    ___ 8. Atrophied   H. Absolute; not to be given up
    ___ 9. Vintage   I. To rid of by or as if by driving away or scattering
    ___ 10. Corroborate   J. Wasted away

VOCABULARY CHAPTERS 13-15 *Travels With Charley*

Part I: Using Prior Knowledge and Contextual Clues

Below are the sentences in which the vocabulary words appear in the text. Read the sentence. Use any clues you can find in the sentence combined with your prior knowledge, and write what you think the underlined words mean on the lines provided.

1. I could hear canned goods crashing as he struggled in his mania. Bears simply brought out the Hyde in my Jekyll-headed dog. . . . No amount of natural wonders, . . . could even engage my attention while that <u>pandemonium</u> went on.

2. We fly it in five hours, drive it in a week, <u>dawdle</u> it as I was doing in a month or six weeks.

3. A few mountain cabins were <u>incised</u> into the steep slopes, but not many.

4. A sound of a quarrel came from the back room . . . . Then a burly man came through the door, still scowling from the <u>fracas</u>.

5. . . . I admitted a young man of about twenty, dressed in gray flannel slacks, two-tone shoes, a polka-dotted ascot, and a blazer with the badge of a Spokane high school His dark, shining hair was a masterpiece of over-combing. . . . He was a shock to me after the <u>ogre</u> of the lunch counter.

6. When I came to my cabin after trying to help Charley in his <u>travail</u> . . . .

7. When the alcoholic vet touched him with his unsteady, <u>inept</u> hand, I saw the look of veiled contempt in Charley's eyes.

8. No car has ever had such <u>obsequious</u> treatment as did Rocinante as we moved slowly on.

Travels With Charley Vocabulary Worksheet Chapters 13-15 Continued

Part II: Determining the Meaning
    Match the vocabulary words to their dictionary definitions

   ___ 1. Pandemonium   A. Anyone especially cruel, brutish, or hideous
   ___ 2. Dawdle   B. Noisy quarrel; brawl
   ___ 3. Incised   C. Clumsy; incompetent
   ___ 4. Fracas   D. Uproar & noise
   ___ 5. Ogre   E. Full of servile compliance; fawning
   ___ 6. Travail   F. Labor
   ___ 7. Inept   G. Cut into
   ___ 8. Obsequious   H. Wasting time lingering

VOCABULARY CHAPTERS 16-21 *Travels With Charley*

Part I: Using Prior Knowledge and Contextual Clues
Below are the sentences in which the vocabulary words appear in the text. Read the sentence. Use any clues you can find in the sentence combined with your prior knowledge, and write what you think the underlined words mean on the lines provided.

1. The experience might even drive him mad. I had thought of that. On the other hand, it might make of him a consummate bore.

    _____

2. The trees rise straight up to zenith; there is no horizon.

    _____

3. No sound of footsteps can be heard on this thick blanket. To me there's a remote and cloistered feeling here. One holds back speech for fear of disturbing something–what?

    _____

4. Can it be that we do not love to be reminded that we are very young and callow in a world that was old when we came into it?

    _____

5. The top is shaved off and a television relay station lunges at the sky and feeds a nervous picture to thousands of tiny houses clustered like aphids beside the roads.

    _____

6, 7. . . . the burden on real estate will be so great that no one will be able to afford it; far from being a source of profit, ownership will be a penalty, and this will be the apex of a pyramid of paradoxes.

    _____

    _____

8. If I found matters to criticize and to deplore, they were tendencies equally present in myself.

    _____

9. California searches vehicles for vegetables and fruits which might carry pernicious insects and diseases.

    _____

Travels With Charley Vocabulary Worksheet Chapters 16-21 Continued

Part II: Determining the Meaning
    Match the vocabulary words to their dictionary definitions

   ____ 1. Consummate   A. Destructive; harmful
   ____ 2. Zenith   B. Immature; inexperienced
   ____ 3. Cloistered   C. Upper region of the sky
   ____ 4. Callow   D. Highest point; culmination
   ____ 5. Aphids   E. Sheltered
   ____ 6. Apex   F. Lament; feel or express sorrow
   ____ 7. Paradox   G. Skilled; perfect
   ____ 8. Deplore   H. Seemingly contradictory statement that may nonetheless be true

   ____ 9. Pernicious   I. Small, soft-bodied insects that suck sap from plants

VOCABULARY CHAPTERS 22-26 *Travels With Charley*

Part I: Using Prior Knowledge and Contextual Clues
Below are the sentences in which the vocabulary words appear in the text. Read the sentence. Use any clues you can find in the sentence combined with your prior knowledge, and write what you think the underlined words mean on the lines provided.

1. The brave bands of Texans did indeed wrest their liberty from Mexico

   _____

2. But no account of Texas would be complete without a Texas orgy, showing men of great wealth squandering their millions on tasteless and impassioned exhibitionism.

   _____

3. And the subtlety of their ostentation drew my attention.

   _____

4. And now I feel better for having exposed to the light of scrutiny the decadent practices of the rich Texans I know.

   _____

5. It all boils down to this: the Americans, the British are that faceless clot you don't know, but a Frenchman or an Italian is your acquaintance and your friend. He has none of the qualities your ignorance causes you to hate. I had always considered this a kind of semantic deadfall.

   _____

6. What made the newsmen love the story was a group of stout middle-aged women who, by some curious definition of the word "mother," gathered every day to scream invectives at children.

   _____

7. I've seen this kind bellow for blood at a prize fight, have orgasms when a man is gored in the bull ring, stare with vicarious lust at a highway accident, stand patiently in line for the privilege of watching any pain or any agony.

   _____

8. Then you must crush his manlike tendencies and make of him the docile beast you want.

   _____

Travels With Charley Vocabulary Worksheet Chapters 22-26 Continued

9. It's true, I <u>goaded</u> him, but I couldn't help it. I guess when they're drafting peacemakers they'd better pass me by.

_____

10. I speculated with a kind of wonder on the strength of the individuality of journeys and stopped on the <u>postulate</u> that people don't take trips–trips take people.

_____

Part II: Determining the Meaning
   Match the vocabulary words to their dictionary definitions

   ___ 1. Wrest   A. Teachable; yielding; able to be formed
   ___ 2. Orgy   B. Experienced through imaginative participation in the
                              experiences of another
   ___ 3. Ostentation   C. Urged; prodded
   ___ 4. Decadent   D. To obtain forcefully
   ___ 5. Semantic   E. Something generally accepted without proof
   ___ 6. Invectives   F. Showiness to impress others
   ___ 7. Vicarious   G. A revel involving unrestrained indulgence
   ___ 8. Docile   H. Relating to language
   ___ 9. Goaded   I. Abusive & insulting language
   ___ 10. Postulate   J. A condition or process of mental or moral decay

VOCABULARY ANSWER KEY *Travels With Charley*

	1-4	5-6	7-8	9-12	13-15	16-21	22-26
1	J	C	D	B	D	G	D
2	D	G	G	E	H	C	G
3	I	D	F	I	G	E	F
4	A	B	B	F	B	B	J
5	K	H	A	H	A	I	H
6	G	K	E	A	F	D	I
7	H	I	C	C	C	H	B
8	E	L		J	E	F	A
9	B	J		D		A	C
10	F	F		G			E
11	C	A					
12		E					

DAILY LESSONS

TEACHER'S NOTE:

This unit is designed so it can be either fifteen or twenty-four lessons long. Lessons sixteen through twenty four are a mini-unit concerned with planning a vacation. This project was one my students really enjoyed, and it is one which gives practical applications of skills learned in English class. *Travels With Charley* provides the perfect opportunity to do this project in conjunction with a literature-based unit.

There are many opportunities in lessons one through fifteen for students to earn "money" which they can apply towards their vacation "budgets." For example, simply assign a "dollar" value to grades received on writing assignments, quizzes, vocabulary work, etc. Give a certain dollar value to class attendance, class participation, oral reading, etc. By doing well in class and on their assignments, students then have more "money" to be able to spend on their vacations. (Likewise, you can also subtract dollars for unwanted behavior and other infractions on your classroom rules.)

Students can do the vacation project alone or in small groups. If a few students want to go on vacation together, they may pool their money and plan a vacation together. In fact, this assignment works best if students do work in small groups of two to four people. Each group must submit a written vacation plan and each individual in the group must submit his/her own Vacation Writing Assignment (Lesson Twenty-One). Each member of the group must participate in the Vacation Project Presentation (lessons twenty-two through twenty four).

If you plan to do the vacation project with your class, it will help considerably if you introduce the project in Lesson One by distributing the Vacation Assignment page and discussing it. Students will then better understand what will be expected of them throughout the unit and can give some thought to the project prior to Lesson Sixteen. Students may also decide to choose a city (for the city assignment made in Lesson Two) which may be included on their vacation project.

When I did this project with my students, I contacted my local AAA office, briefly explained the project to the travel agent and asked if AAA could help by donating some current (within the last year or two) guide books, maps, etc. so students would have a good supply of materials with which to work in the classroom. AAA responded by donating a couple of complete sets of tour books some US road maps, and other useful information. You might be able to get a whole bunch of materials if you contact AAA when they are ready to discard the previous year's excess supply of materials. I then saved the materials they donated, and used them for several years.

For more details, see lessons sixteen through twenty-four.

LESSON ONE

Objectives
1. To introduce the *Travels With Charley* unit
2. To distribute books, study guides and other related materials

NOTE: Prior to this lesson, go to your local travel agency, library, or video store to find a travelogue of America. Try to find one that gives information about a wide variety of things to see and do in America (as opposed to one just about national parks, only about the Grand Canyon, or any other particular point of interest.)

If no film is available (or if you prefer not to use a film), a good alternative activity is to have prepared a bulletin board titled GETTING ACQUAINTED WITH AMERICA on which you have posted a collage of pictures of points of interest in America. Use that bulletin board as a starting point for a discussion about all the things the U. S. Has to offer. Ask your students where they have traveled in the United States, where else they have lived, or what things they have heard about that they would like to see.

Activity #1
Show the film or hold a discussion as directed above. Make the transition to the book by noting that the book students are about to read is a story about a man who traveled across the United States with his dog, Charley.

Activity #2
Distribute the materials students will use in this unit. Explain in detail how students are to use these materials.

Study Guides   Students should read the study guide questions for each reading assignment prior to beginning the reading assignment to get a feeling for what events and ideas are important in the section they are about to read. After reading the section, students will (as a class or individually) answer the questions to review the important events and ideas from that section of the book. Students should keep the study guides as study materials for the unit test.

Vocabulary   Prior to reading a reading assignment, students will do vocabulary work related to the section of the book they are about to read. Following the completion of the reading of the book, there will be a vocabulary review of all the words used in the vocabulary assignments. Students should keep their vocabulary work as study materials for the unit test.

Reading Assignment Sheet   You need to fill in the reading assignment sheet to let students know by when their reading has to be completed. You can either write the assignment sheet up on a side blackboard or bulletin board and leave it there for students to see each day, or you can "ditto" copies for each student to have. In either case, you should advise students to become very familiar with the reading assignments so they know what is expected of them.

Extra Activities Center The Unit Resource Materials portion of this LitPlan contains suggestions for an extra library of related books and articles in your classroom as well as crossword and word search puzzles. Make an extra activities center in your room where you will keep these materials for students to use. (Bring the books and articles in from the library and keep several copies of the puzzles on hand.) Explain to students that these materials are available for students to use when they finish reading assignments or other class work early.

Nonfiction Assignment Sheet Explain to students that they each are to read at least one non-fiction piece from the in-class library at some time during the unit. Students will fill out a nonfiction assignment sheet after completing the reading to help you (the teacher) evaluate their reading experiences and to help the students think about and evaluate their own reading experiences.

Books Each school has its own rules and regulations regarding student use of school books. Advise students of the procedures that are normal for your school. Preview the book. Look at the covers, frontmatter, and index. Glance through at some of the drawings.

NONFICTION ASSIGNMENT SHEET
(To be completed after reading the required nonfiction article)

Name _____ Date _____

Title of Nonfiction Read _____

Written By _____ Publication Date _____

I. Factual Summary: Write a short summary of the piece you read.

II. Vocabulary
    1. With which vocabulary words in the piece did you encounter some degree of difficulty?

    2. How did you resolve your lack of understanding with these words?

III. Interpretation: What was the main point the author wanted you to get from reading his work?

IV. Criticism
    1. With which points of the piece did you agree or find easy to accept? Why?

    2. With which points of the piece did you disagree or find difficult to believe? Why?

V. Personal Response: What do you think about this piece? OR How does this piece influence your ideas?

LESSON TWO

Objectives:
1. To have students learn about other towns and cities in the U.S.
2. To help students gather information for their city reports
3. To introduce Writing Assignment #1: Writing To Inform

Activity 1

Distribute the City Report Assignments. Discuss the directions in detail.

NOTE: If you have all students fill out a worksheet (included with the assignment) to be handed in with the written report, you can compile all of the worksheets into a booklet, a "Guide to Cities of the U.S.," and distribute a copy to each student who would like to have one. That makes a fun (and useful) conclusion to the project.

Activity 2

Have your students orally brainstorm a list of major cities in the USA. Write the list so students can see it as they progress. If they have difficulty, pull down a map of the United States or ask for cities in particular states. As they create the list, ask if anyone knows anything about the cities being named.

Activity 3

After the list is created, give students a few minutes to think about what cities they want to investigate for their City Projects. Tell each student to write his/her name on a piece of paper along with the name of the city he/she has chosen to research. Quickly have each student state the city of his/her choice orally. You may or may not want to eliminate duplicates. If you live in a major city, you may want to eliminate that to force students to look beyond their own back doors.

Activity 4

If time remains in the class, students should write down anything they know or think they know about the city they have chosen. You may or may not want to collect the name/city papers so you have a record what each student is doing and/or to hand them back to the students at the end of the project to see if what they thought they knew about the city was correct.

CITY REPORT ASSIGNMENT

Steinbeck travels across the United States and records his thoughts about each of the main places he visits. Too often we tend to forget the diverse nature of our country and we take for granted the variety of experiences available in the various regions of our nation.

Your assignment is to choose a city or town in the United States and to prepare full written and oral presentations about that city or town. Your report should include (but is not limited to) location, transportation available in and around the city, industry, arts/entertainment available there, history, sights to see (parks, landmarks, museums, etc.), schools and universities, weather, mayor's name, current issues in the city, sports teams, and the advantages and disadvantages of living in that city. Your oral presentation to the class should have some visual aids (pictures, drawings, maps and/or slides, etc.). Consider making a power point presentation.

There are many ways to gather information about the city you have chosen. Most cities have a web page which will have a lot of information. Most cities also have a chamber of commerce you can email or call to get more or printed information. Travel agencies and the library are also good sources. Use at least two different sources to gather information.

Use the writing assignment page to help you organize and prepare your written report. You will not read your report for your oral presentation, but you may make notes from your written report to remind you of what you want to say in your oral presentation. Your oral presentation should last no less than five minutes and no more than seven minutes. It should also include some visual aids like maps, posters, pictures, etc. You will be penalized on your grade if you take more or less than the allotted time.

BASIC FACTS ABOUT _____
(city's name)

LOCATION

WEATHER

HISTORY

TRANSPORTATION

INDUSTRY/ECONOMY

ENTERTAINMENT

SPORTS

SIGHTS TO SEE

SCHOOLS/UNIVERSITIES

MAYOR/PROMINENT CITY OFFICIALS

CURRENT ISSUES

MISCELLANEOUS INFORMATION (Use the back of this page.)

WRITING ASSIGNMENT 1 *Travels With Charley*
Writing To Inform

PROMPT
Travels With Charley is in its own way a big informative essay. Steinbeck informs us of what he found in his travels across America. He didn't travel to every city, and, certainly, cities have changed since he wrote this book. Even his home town had changed in the number of years it had been since he had been there. Your project is to look at just one city but to do so in detail. If everyone in the class picks a different city and shares the information with everyone else in class, we will have a new portrait of urban America. Although your report won't be written as an informative travelogue, you can make the report interesting to read–not just a list of facts and figures.

PREWRITING
Gather your facts together for each of the categories listed. That may mean simply reorganizing note cards or pieces of paper; it may mean reorganizing your facts in a word processing program; it may mean rewriting your facts on one page for each topic. Look at your facts within each category. Eliminate facts that are duplicated. Try to see what the most logical order of presentation would be to make the ideas flow from one to another. Number or reorganize your facts into this order. Now, in what order would the categories you have flow best? Reorganize the categories into that order.

DRAFTING
Your final, written report should have an introduction and should be clearly organized into sections for each of the required categories of information (and any other categories you feel are appropriate to add for your particular city). Include any appropriate drawings, maps or pictures in your written report. Try to think of an interesting way to present your facts rather than just writing them all in simple sentences. Your report should also have a concluding section. In your conclusion, give your own thoughts about the information you have found, your thoughts about the city.

PROMPT
When you finish the rough draft of your composition, ask a student who sits near you to read it. After reading your rough draft, he/she should tell you what he/she liked best about your work, which parts were difficult to understand, and ways in which your work could be improved. Reread your paper considering your critic's comments, and make the corrections you think are necessary. Ask your classmate what he/she thought of each of the characters/events you chose for your assignment.

PROOFREADING
Do a final proofreading of your paper double-checking your grammar, spelling, organization, and the clarity of your ideas.

LESSON THREE

<u>Objectives</u>
1. To show students how to do the pre-reading work for each reading assignment
2. To read chapters 1-4
3. To evluate students' oral reading

<u>Activity 1</u>
Tell students to look their *Travels With Charley* study questions for the first reading assignment. Explain that before reading each assignment, they should read over the study questions to familiarize themselves with what kinds of things will happen in these chapters and to key in on the events or ideas of importance.

<u>Activity 2</u>
Tell students to look at their vocabulary worksheets for the first reading assignment. Explain that prior to each reading assignment, one of these vocabulary worksheets will be completed. Explain the directions in detail and give students time to complete the assignment. After students have completed the worksheet, give the answers to Part II so they have the correct definitions.

<u>Activity 3</u>
Have students read Chapters 1-4 of *Travels With Charley* out loud in class. You probably know the best way to get readers with your class; pick students at random, ask for volunteers, or use whatever method works best for your group. If you have not yet completed an oral reading evaluation for your students this period, this would be a good opportunity to do so. A form is included with this unit for your convenience. If students don't complete the reading assignment in class, they should do so on their own prior to the next class period.

ORAL READING EVALUATION *Travels With Charley*

Name _____ Class____ Date _____

SKILL	EXCELLENT	GOOD	AVERAGE	FAIR	POOR
Fluency	5	4	3	2	1
Clarity	5	4	3	2	1
Audibility	5	4	3	2	1
Pronunciation	5	4	3	2	1
_____	5	4	3	2	1
_____	5	4	3	2	1

Total _____   Grade _____

Comments:

LESSON FOUR

Objectives
   1. To review the main events and ideas of the first reading assignment ("chapters" 1-4)
   2. To do the pre-reading work for and complete reading assignment 2 ("chapters" 5-6)

Activity #1
Give students a few minutes to formulate answers for the study guide questions for the first reading assignment, and then discuss the answers to the questions in detail. Write the answers on the board or overhead transparency so students can have the correct answers for study purposes. Note: It is a good practice in public speaking and leadership skills for individual students to take charge of leading the discussions of the study questions. Perhaps a different student could go to the front of the class and lead the discussion each day that the study questions are discussed during this unit. Of course, the teacher should guide the discussion when appropriate and be sure to fill in any gaps the students leave.

Activity #2
Tell students to read over the study questions for the next reading assignment ("chapters" 5-6) and complete the related vocabulary worksheet.

Activity #2
Have students read "chapters" 5-6 of *Travels With Charley* out loud in class. Continue with the oral reading evaluations. If students do not complete reading this section, they should do so prior to the next class meeting.

LESSON FIVE

Objectives
- 1. To review the main events and ideas of the second reading assignment ("chapters" 5-6)
- 2. To do the pre-reading work for and complete reading assignment 3 ("chapters" 7-8)

Activity #1
Give students a few minutes to formulate answers for the study guide questions for the second reading assignment, and then discuss the answers to the questions in detail. Write the answers on the board or overhead transparency so students can have the correct answers for study purposes.

Activity #2
Tell students to read over the study questions for the next reading assignment ("chapters" 7-8) and complete the related vocabulary worksheet. After students are finished, give them the answers to Part II so they have the correct definitions to study.

Activity #2
Have students read "chapters" 7-8 of *Travels With Charley* out loud in class. Continue with the oral reading evaluations. If you have completed the oral reading assignments, students may read silently during this class period. If students do not complete reading this section, they should do so prior to the next class meeting.

LESSON SIX

<u>Objectives</u>
    1. To check students' reading comprehension of reading assignment 3 ("chapters" 7-8)
    2. To give students the opportunity to do research for their city reports
    3. To help students become more familiar with the many resources available in the library

<u>Activity 1</u>
Distribute the multiple choice quiz questions for reading assignment 3 ("chapters" 7-8). Give students ample time to complete the quizzes. Have students swap papers for grading, and discuss the answers in detail. Be sure students fill in the correct answers for anything that is wrong, so the test taker will have the correct answers to study from. Collect the papers if you want to record the grades.

<u>Activity 2</u>
Take your class to the school library so they can do some of the necessary research for their city reports. Have the librarian (or you can) show students the best places to look for information about their cities. Be sure to note the periodicals for information about the current issues facing the cities. Note also the places in your library where visual aids might be found. Students should use the remainder of this class period to find and read information related to their cities. They also could use this time to complete the Nonfiction Assignment Sheet if you want students to do those during this unit.

LESSON SEVEN

<u>Objectives</u>
    1. To preview reading assignment 4 ("chapters" 9-12) by reviewing the study questions and doing the vocabulary worksheets
    2. To read assignment 4

<u>Activity</u>
Give students ample time to preview the study questions and do the vocabulary worksheets for reading assignment 4. Discuss the answers to Part II of the vocabulary so students have the correct answers to study. When that is completed, students should spend the remainder of the class reading assignment 4 and should complete it prior to the next class meeting.

LESSON EIGHT

Objectives
>   1. To review the main events and ideas from reading assignment 4 ("chapters"9-12)
>   2. Students will practice creative writing while showing an understanding of Steinbeck and his journey

Activity #1
Review the main events and ideas from reading assignment 4 by discussing the answers to the study questions for that section of the book as directed previously.

Activity #2
Distribute Writing Assignment 2 and discuss the directions in detail. Give students the remainder of the class period to complete this assignment.

LESSON NINE

Objective
>   To preview and read assignment 5 ("chapters" 13-15)

Activity
Give students ample time to preview the study questions and do the vocabulary worksheets for reading assignment 5. Discuss the answers to Part II of the vocabulary so students have the correct answers to study. When that is completed, students should spend the remainder of the class reading assignment 5 and should complete it prior to the next class meeting.

WRITING ASSIGNMENT 2 Travels With Charley
Creative Writing/Personal Opinion

PROMPT
We have been reading John Steinbeck's account of his travels in America. By now you should have an understanding of his writing style and the kinds of things he does. Your assignment is to write an episode of Steinbeck's travels as he would have written it. Make up a ficticious day or evening in Steinbeck's travels and write it down.

PREWRITING
Working with your partner, decide on when and where the episode will take place and sketch out what events will happen. Discuss things Steinbeck might say relating to the episode. Make an outline of roughly how you think things would go. You may expand on an episode or event he actually uses in the book or think of something entirely different.

DRAFTING
Using your outline, write out the actual paragraphs and dialogue for the episode. Both partners need to work on this assignment to try to get the actual feel of one of Steinbeck's entries. Brainstorm and make suggestions about word choices and phrasing to try to fit the feel of *Travels With Charley*.

PROMPT
When you finish the rough draft of your composition, ask a student who sits near you to read it. After reading your rough draft, he/she should tell you what he/she liked best about your work, which parts were difficult to understand, and ways in which your work could be improved. Reread your paper considering your critic's comments, and make the corrections you think are necessary. Ask your classmate what he/she thought of each of the characters/events you chose for your assignment.

PROOFREADING
Do a final proofreading of your paper double-checking your grammar, spelling, organization, and the clarity of your ideas.

WRITING EVALUATION FORM - *Travels With Charley*

Name _____ Date _____

Grade _____

Circle One For Each Item:

Grammar:	correct	errors noted on paper
Spelling:	correct	errors noted on paper
Punctuation:	correct	errors noted on paper
Legibility:	excellent	good fair poor
_____	excellent	good fair poor
_____	excellent	good fair poor

Strengths:

Weaknesses:

LESSON TEN

Objectives
    1. To review the main events and ideas from reading assignment 5 ("chapters"13-15)
    2. To give student time to work on their city projects
    3. To preview and read assignment 6 ("chapters" 16-21)

Activity #1
Review the main events and ideas from reading assignment 5 by discussing the answers to the study questions for that section of the book as directed previously.

Activity #2
Give students most of the class period to work on their city project assignments. Circulate around the room offering help and checking on students' progress.

Activity #3
Tell students that prior to the next class period they should have completed the pre-reading work and reading of assignment 6 ("chapters" 16-21). If students finish with their city project work before the end of class, they should start on this assignment.

LESSON ELEVEN

Objectives
    1. To review the main ideas and events from reading assignment 6 ("chapters" 16-21)
    2. To read assignment 7 ("chapters" 22-26)

Activity #1
Review the main events and ideas from reading assignment 6 by discussing the answers to the study questions for that section of the book as directed previously. If you feel students need a quiz at this point, use the multiple choice study questions as a quiz and discuss the answers in detail.

Activity #2
Give students ample time to preview the study questions and do the vocabulary worksheets for reading assignment 7. Discuss the answers to Part II of the vocabulary so students have the correct answers to study. When that is completed, students should spend the remainder of the class reading assignment 7 and should complete it prior to the next class meeting.

LESSON TWELVE

Objectives
    1. To review the main events and ideas of reading assignment 7 ("chapters" 22-26)
    2. Students will practice writing to persuade

Activity 1
Review the events of the last reading assignment by discussing the study questions in detail. Ask if students have any questions about any of the study questions from any of the book. Give students about 15 minutes to work with classmates to repair any missing or wrong study answers.

Activity 2
    Distribute Writing Assignment 3. Discuss the directions in detail and give students ample time to complete the assignment.

LESSONS THIRTEEN AND FOURTEEN

Objectives
    1. To bring to culmination the city projects
    2. Students will practice public speaking
    3. Students will be exposed to information about many U.S. cities

Activity
In whatever order you determine, have students each get up in front of the class and present their city projects. Allow a minute or two for any questions from classmates after the presentation. Grade the projects on your own criteria, though an evaluation form is enclosed for your convenience. Students should hand in their completed reports and materials after their presentations are completed.

WRITING ASSIGNMENT 3 - *Travels With Charley*

PROMPT
Steinbeck spent a relatively short time in New Orleans, but he had a lot to say about it. The "Cheerleaders" were particularly upsetting. Your assignment is to pretend you are John Steinbeck in New Orleans, confronting a Cheerleader and persuading her to change her attitude. Write the episode as you believe it could have happened.

PREWRITING
What are the most compelling things Steinbeck could say to the Cheerleader to make her change? Brainstorm as many ideas as you can think of and jot them down on paper. Seriously look at your points. Which 3 are the strongest, the most likely to succeed? How would he go about bringing up the points, and what would he say about each? Jot down your ideas. Now, in your mind see Mr. Steinbeck going up to one of those Cheerleaders and talking to her. What is his approach? In what way would he convey his 3 strongest points? What will the reaction of the Cheerleader be? Write down what you think.

DRAFTING
Looking at all your notes, outline the episode and write it as an entry in *Travels With Charley*. You've already had a little practice in writing an episode. This time you have the added burden of persuasion. Make the episode as realistic as possible.

PROMPT
When you finish the rough draft of your composition, ask a student who sits near you to read it. After reading your rough draft, he/she should tell you what he/she liked best about your work, which parts were difficult to understand, and ways in which your work could be improved. Reread your paper considering your critic's comments, and make the corrections you think are necessary. Ask your classmate what he/she thought of each of the characters/events you chose for your assignment.

PROOFREADING
Do a final proofreading of your paper double-checking your grammar, spelling, organization, and the clarity of your ideas.

CITY REPORT PRESENTATION EVALUATION

Name _____ Date _____ Grade _____

City Assigned _____

End Time ___:___
Begin Time ___:___
Total Time ___:___

	A	B	C	D	E
Time	1	2	3	4	5
Content	1	2	3	4	5
Clarity	1	2	3	4	5
Volume	1	2	3	4	5
Visuals	1	2	3	4	5
Organization	1	2	3	4	5
Enthusiasm	1	2	3	4	5
_____	1	2	3	4	5
_____	1	2	3	4	5

Total _____

Comments:

LESSONS FIFTEEN AND SIXTEEN

Objective
To discuss the book in greater depth

Activity
Have students answer the questions on the Extra Discussion Questions/Writing Assignments sheet in this packet. Entering into a discussion of this kind "cold" is sometimes difficult. One quick way to overcome this problem is to assign one question to each student and allow students to have about 10 minutes to formulate answers to their questions. Each student should then be ready to lead or at least begin a discussion of one question.

Have students take notes during this session. (If your students need it, a review of note-taking skills might be appropriate as a lesson prior to this one.) You may wish to help them identify the important ideas by jotting down "notes" on the board. If you want to have a more spontaneous discussion, I suggest that you eliminate the "note-taking" portion of the activity and give students a "hand-out" with the "answers" to the questions after the discussion. (I prefer to have students take their own notes and to take the time to check their notes, but if you are rushed for time for some reason, the latter is an alternative way of doing this activity.)

EXTRA WRITING ASSIGNMENTS AND/OR DISCUSSION QUESTIONS
Travels With Charley

<u>Interpretive</u>

1. Why did Steinbeck take this journey across America?

2. If the story had been written from Charley's point of view, how would that have changed the story and its effect?

3. Why did Steinbeck feel he needed to conceal his identity during his trip?

4. What is the significance of the name Rocinante?

5. What are "stereotypes"? Are the people Steinbeck mentions stereotypical? Why or why not?

6. Describe Steinbeck's writing style.

7. *Travels With Charley* is a short book. Could anything have been gained by including more scenes from Steinbeck's journey? If so, what could have been added and for what purpose? If not, explain why not.

8. Describe Steinbeck's feelings about hunting. Do you agree?

9. Steinbeck uses Charley as an "icebreaker" with strangers. What other methods do people use to meet or talk with strangers?

10. Steinbeck preferred secondary roads over the super-highways. He felt you could see, hear and smell America on the smaller roads. He also felt that you passed over America on the super-highways. Did his observations of the long distance truckers support this theory? If so, how?

11. In what ways are the mobile homes and trailer parks mirrors of our society?

Travels With Charley Extra Discussion Questions Page 2

Critical

12. Explain, "for a man has to have feelings and then words before he can come close to thought."

13. Describe John Steinbeck. What kind of a man is he?

14. Steinbeck observed that Americans had put cleanliness first at the expense of taste. The sense of taste then disappears and any tastes that are strong, pungent or exotic cause suspicion. To what else besides food was he referring?

15. Upon returning to Monterey, why did Steinbeck agree with Thomas Wolfe's book "You Can't Go Home Again"? Do you agree?

16. Explain Steinbeck's reasons he was unable to find the truth about his country during his trip.

17. What did Steinbeck mean when he wrote, "the South is in the pain of labor with the nature of its future child still unknown"?

18. Why did Steinbeck say that Texas was considered a state of mind?

19. In what ways are all Americans similar? How do they differ?

20. What are the main conflicts in the story, and how is each resolved?

21. Was Charley a good traveling companion? Would a person have been a better choice? Why or why not?

22. In what ways were Steinbeck's perceptions of Black Americans influenced by his childhood?

23. Compare and contrast the four southern men Steinbeck met outside of New Orleans: the gentlemen, the old Negro farmer, the white racist, and the Negro college student.

24. Summarize Steinbeck's travels. What does it all boil down to in the end?

Travels With Charley Extra Discussion Questions Page 3

Personal Opinion

25. Steinbeck describes the trash and waste surrounding the cities and wonders if a time will come when we cannot afford our own wastefulness. Has this become a fact? If so, what is being done to remedy the situation?

26. Have you ever witnessed someone like a Cheerleader, hurling invectives against an innocent person? What was your reaction? Did you get involved? Why or why not?

27. Would you like to take a journey and see the country and its people the way Steinbeck did? Why or why not?

28. How would Steinbeck's trip be different today?

LESSON SEVENTEEN

Objective
To review all of the vocabulary work done in this unit

Activity
Choose one (or more) of the vocabulary review activities listed below and spend your class period as directed in the activity. Some of the materials for these review activities are located in the Vocabulary Resource Materials section in this LitPlan.

VOCABULARY REVIEW ACTIVITIES

1. Divide your class into two teams and have an old-fashioned spelling or definition bee.

2. Give each of your students (or students in groups of two, three or four) an *Travels With Charley* Vocabulary Word Search Puzzle. The person (group) to find all of the vocabulary words in the puzzle first wins.

3. Give students an *Travels With Charley* Vocabulary Word Search Puzzle without the word list. The person or group to find the most vocabulary words in the puzzle wins.

4. Use an *Travels With Charley* Vocabulary Crossword Puzzle. Put the puzzle onto a transparency on the overhead projector (so everyone can see it), and do the puzzle together as a class.

5. Give students an *Travels With Charley* Vocabulary Matching Worksheet to do.

6. Divide your class into two teams. Use *Travels With Charley* vocabulary words with their letters jumbled as a word list. Student 1 from Team A faces off against Student 1 from Team B. You write the first jumbled word on the board. The first student (1A or 1B) to unscramble the word wins the chance for his/her team to score points. If 1A wins the jumble, go to student 2A and give him/her a definition. He/she must give you the correct spelling of the vocabulary word which fits that definition. If he/she does, Team A scores a point, and you give student 3A a definition for which you expect a correctly spelled matching vocabulary word. Continue giving Team A definitions until some team member makes an incorrect response. An incorrect response sends the game back to the jumbled-word face off, this time with students 2A and 2B. Instead of repeating giving definitions to the first few students of each team, continue with the student after the one who gave the last incorrect response on the team. For example, if Team B wins the jumbled-word face-off, and student 5B gave the last incorrect answer for Team B, you would start this round of definition questions with student 6B, and so on. The team with the most points wins!

7. Have students write a story in which they correctly use as many vocabulary words as possible. Have students read their compositions orally! Post the most original compositions on your bulletin board!

LESSON EIGHTEEN

Objective
> To review the main ideas and events in *Travels With Charley*

Activity
Choose one of the review games/activities suggested in this unit and spend your class time as directed there.

REVIEW GAMES/ACTIVITIES *Travels With Charley*

1. Ask the class to make up a unit test for *Travels With Charley*. The test should have 4 sections: matching, true/false, short answer, and essay. Students may use 1/2 period to make the test and then swap papers and use the other 1/2 class period to take a test a classmate has devised. (open book) You may want to use the unit test included in this packet or take questions from the students' unit tests to formulate your own test.

2. Take 1/2 period for students to make up true and false questions (including the answers). Collect the papers and divide the class into two teams. Draw a big tic-tac-toe board on the chalk board. Make one team X and one team O. Ask questions to each side, giving each student one turn. If the question is answered correctly, that students' team's letter (X or O) is placed in the box. If the answer is incorrect, no letter is placed in the box. The object is to get three in a row like tic-tac-toe. You may want to keep track of the number of games won for each team.

3. Take 1/2 period for students to make up questions (true/false and short answer). Collect the questions. Divide the class into two teams. You'll alternate asking questions to individual members of teams A & B (like in a spelling bee). The question keeps going from A to B until it is correctly answered, then a new question is asked. A correct answer does not allow the team to get another question. Correct answers are +2 points; incorrect answers are -1 point.

4. Have students pair up and quiz each other from their study guides and class notes.

5. Give students an *Travels With Charley* crossword puzzle to complete.

6. Divide your class into two teams. Use *Travels With Charley* crossword words with their letters jumbled as a word list. Student 1 from Team A faces off against Student 1 from Team B. You write the first jumbled word on the board. The first student (1A or 1B) to unscramble the word wins the chance for his/her team to score points. If 1A wins the jumble, go to student 2A and give him/her a clue. He/she must give you the correct word which matches that clue. If he/she does, Team A scores a point, and you give student 3A a clue for which you expect another correct response. Continue giving Team A clues until some team member makes an incorrect response. An incorrect response sends the game back to the jumbled-word face off, this time with students 2A and 2B. Instead of repeating giving clues to the first few students of each team, continue with the student after the one who gave the last incorrect response on the team. For example, if Team B wins the jumbled-word face-off, and student 5B gave the last incorrect answer for Team B, you would start this round of clue questions with student 6B, and so on. The team with the most points wins!

Review Games Page 2

8. Play What's My Line?. This is similar to the old television show. Students assume the roles of different characters from the epic. One student gives clues to the class, or to a panel of contestants. The contestants try to guess the identity of the guest. Students may enjoy assisting you in creating rules and procedures for the game.

9. Play Jeopardy. Divide the class into two groups. Assign each group a category or book from the epic and have them devise answers for that category. Play the game according to the television show procedures.

10. Play Drawing in the Details. This is similar to Pictionary. Divide students into teams. A student from one team draws a scene from the epic. (You may want to specify the Book or section.) Drawings should be kept simple, to keep the pace lively. Students in the opposing team locate the scene in their books and read it aloud. If they are incorrect, the illustrator's team has a chance to guess. Involve students in setting up a scoring system and any other necessary rules.

NOTE: The following lessons are an optional vacation project. If you wish to use them, do so after the unit test for *Travels With Charley*.

LESSON TWENTY (after the test)

Objectives
      1. To introduce the vacation project
      2. To have students make a practical application of skills learned in English class
        (researching, organizing, writing, thinking)

Activity #1
Have a travel agent come in to class to talk about the things one must consider and do to plan a successful vacation. You might ask the agent to try to tie in with your assignment by mentioning several of the items on the students' assignment list.

Activity #2
Make the vacation project assignment; distribute the assignment papers and discuss the directions in detail.

VACATION ASSIGNMENT *Travels With Charley*

Steinbeck took a great deal of time to plan his trip across America. When we take a vacation, we need to make similar preparations. Your assignment is to plan a vacation.

PART ONE:
In the unit about *Travels With Charley* you have earned "money" by completing the assignments and classwork.

PART TWO:
Now, the money you earned is your budget for your vacation. If you earned a lot of money, you can take an extravagant vacation. If you don't have a lot of money, you have to figure out how to have a nice vacation on a budget.

You may go on a vacation alone or you may get together with a friend or two, pool your money, and take a trip together.

In Part Two of this assignment, you will produce a Vacation Plan in which you give the exact details you plan for your vacation. (See Vacation Plan Worksheet.)

PART THREE:
After you have planned your vacation, you will take time to think about what kinds of things you did and what kinds of adventures you had on your vacation. If you took a group vacation, you need to get together with your fellow travelers and fabricate your trip. After actually imagining your vacation, you will write a composition telling about your vacation. (See Vacation Writing Assignment.)

PART FOUR:
After you have planned and "gone on" your vacation, you will make a presentation to the class, giving a little travelogue, telling about your vacation. (See Vacation Presentation.)

VACATION PLAN WORKSHEET

When you plan a vacation, there are certain logical steps to take to insure your vacation will run smoothly. Follow these steps when planning your vacation.

Step One: Decide how much money you have to work with.

Step Two: Decide upon the purpose of your vacation. Is it strictly to have fun? Do you want to learn anything on your vacation? Do you want to "get away from it all" and relax? Is your purpose to do things you don't get a chance to do everyday? Are you looking for a different place to live? Are you traveling just because you want to see something different? The list of possible purposes for a vacation or a trip is endless. What is your purpose?

Step Three: Decide upon the kind of a vacation which will best fulfill your purpose. Do you want to stop at a lot of different places as you travel along, or do you want to get somewhere quickly and use your time there, rather than in travel? Will you be primarily interested in cities or countryside? Do you want amusements and entertainment or historical sites and landmarks?

Step Four: Do some research to see what is available. Once you know the basic kind of a vacation you want, look into all the possibilities for that kind of a vacation. What areas of the country offer what you are looking for? Do you want/need to travel abroad? Where are the most likely places for you to be able to fulfill your vacation's purposes?

Step Five: Begin to consider your budget. Now that you know the kinds of places and things that are available to do, decide the best general way to fulfill your vacation's purpose within your budget. For example, if you only have $200 to spend, you obviously cannot travel abroad. Begin to focus on real possibilities for your vacation within your budget. What general plan do you think you can afford?

Step Six: Get down to the details. Here is where you have to make some definite decisions about length of your vacation (days, weeks), travel arrangements (plane fares, motel/hotel costs, how many miles to drive during the day, etc.), your daily plans (see the museum, rent a boat, see a show,etc.), and other details of your trip (what and when to eat, what to take along, etc). You must find out exactly what everything will cost and consider your priorities. (You may have enough money to go see a show, but you may need to have a cheap dinner instead of going to an expensive, fancy restaurant. You may need to go to cheap motels instead of the more expensive ones. A good way to get through this step is to split up the work load if you are going on a group vacation. Have one person responsible for finding out about hotel/motel/campground rates, someone else responsible for entrance fees, ticket costs, etc., and so on.

Vacation Plan Worksheet (continued)

Step Seven: Get and stay organized. Make a chart (or keep a sheet of paper) for each day of your vacation. Jot down a rough plan for what you plan to do each day (including approximate costs). You will probably scratch and scribble all over this chart by the time you have finalized all of your plans.

Step Eight: Make your reservations. Whenever possible, make your reservations for hotels/motels/campgrounds, shows, dinners, etc. It is best to do this by phone and to follow up with a letter to confirm your phone conversation. (For this assignment, write down the phone number you would call and write out a letter of confirmation for each reservation.) Be sure to find out the cancellation policy in case you need to cancel your reservations. Some things may be better left without reservations until the day or two before if you are on a flexible schedule.

Step Nine: Make final preparations. Decide what to pack. Think about any obligations you have at home in case you need to make arrangements concerning them. If you are going on a group vacation, consider "who will bring what" if need be. (For example, three girls traveling together could save space if necessary by bringing one hair dryer. If you are going on a camping trip, each person could be responsible for bringing certain necessary articles, etc.)

Step Ten: Write down your final Vacation Plan. Include:
    a. name(s) of traveler(s)
    b. purpose of the vacation
    c. budget showing and totaling expenses
    d. packing list, list of responsibilities (for group vacations)
    e. reservation confirmation letter(s)
    f. detailed plan for each day (who, what, when, where, how much cost)
    g. include any graphics which are important to your trip (example: route to drive)

VACATION WRITING ASSIGNMENT

You have planned every detail of your vacation. Now, it is time to be really creative. Think about your plans and imagine every step of your vacation. If you took a group vacation, discuss possibilities of what happened on the vacation with your fellow travelers. Fabricate the entire vacation experience. Remember that things don't always go as planned. What interesting things happened to you on your vacation? Have fun imagining your vacation world!

After you have fabricated your vacation, it is your assignment to WRITE A COMPOSITION ABOUT YOUR VACATION. You may either write a general composition about the nature of the entire vacation giving chronological highlights of your trip, or you may describe some specific incident which happened to you or a member of your group.

Each member of the group must write a composition from his/her own point of view. Each member of the group may NOT write the "same" composition.

VACATION PROJECT PRESENTATIONS

You have planned and taken your vacation. Now it is time for you to share your vacation with everyone else in the class. Using visual aids, you (your group) will make an oral presentation about your vacation to the class.

Give a brief introduction in which you explain your purpose for the vacation and the budget limitations under which you were working.

Tell about your vacation using visual aids.
    a. You may find pictures or slides of things you saw on your vacation.
    b. You may take photos or slides to show the class (by creating scenes from your vacation with the people involved)
    c. You may draw pictures or other graphics which will help to show the class various aspects of your vacation
    d. You may wish to make a model to show some aspect of your vacation
    e. You may create "souvenirs" to show the class

You will be graded on how well you communicate your created vacation to the class, your use of visual aids, your style of presentation, and your creativity.

LESSONS TWENTY-ONE THROUGH TWENTY-FOUR

Objective
    To give students time to do Part Two of the vacation assignment

Activity
Give students this class time to work on Part Two of their vacation projects. Make as many resources as possible available to students in the classroom, and write passes to the library or media room as students may need them to gather information.

Four class periods have been allowed for this work. Depending on the level and ambition of your particular class, you may need more or less time. Judge your own schedule accordingly.

LESSON TWENTY-FIVE

Objectives
    1. To stimulate students' thinking and creativity
    2. To help students visualize something they may only have read about
    3. To set students up for the vacation presentations

Activity
Distribute the Vacation Writing Assignment sheets. Discuss the directions in detail and give students this class period to do the assignment. (See page 51 of this unit plan.)

NOTE: I have allowed one class period for this assignment. Again, your class may need more time to complete it, depending primarily on how much they "get into" the assignment and on their own writing skills. Again use your best judgement when assigning a time when the compositions will be due for grading.

LESSON TWENTY-SIX

Objectives
1. To complete the Vacation Writing Assignments
2. To make the Vacation Presentation Assignment
3. To give students time to work on these assignments

Activity #1
If you feel your students need more time to work on the Vacation Writing Assignment, let them continue working on that.

Activity #2
Distribute the Vacation Project Assignment sheets. Discuss the directions in detail and allow students ample time to complete the work. (See page 52 of this unit plan.)

NOTE: Yet once again, "ample time" will vary from class to class. To get some quality presentations, I would suggest that you make the assignment today and give students about a week before you expect them to make the presentations to the class (lessons twenty-three and twenty-four).

Perhaps if you are going on to another literature unit, you could begin reading the work and take a break for a couple of days in the middle to do these presentations.

LESSONS TWENTY-SEVEN AND TWENTY-EIGHT

Objectives
1. To give students the chance to practice public speaking
2. To draw the vacation projects to a complete conclusion
3. To give students the opportunity to show off their work from the last few weeks so they feel a sense of pride and accomplishment
4. To have some fun and provide some comic relief in the English class

Activity
Have students give their vacation presentations to the class. I have allowed two class periods for this activity, but, again, the actual time needed will depend on your students and you.

UNIT TESTS

SHORT ANSWER UNIT TEST 1 *Travels With Charley*

1. Matching/Identification

_____ 1. Rocinante   A. work of an evil child

_____ 2. Charley   B. reminder of Avalon

_____ 3. Fayre Eleyne   C. wife visited author here

_____ 4. Bad Lands   D. author's birthplace

_____ 5. Deer Isle   E. journey's beginning

_____ 6. Sag Harbor   F. a state of mind

_____ 7. Mojave Desert   G. dog

_____ 8. Texas   H. forced the will to survive

_____ 9. Chicago   I. truck

_____ 10. Salinas   J. boat

II. Short Answer

1. What did Steinbeck see in the eyes of many of the people he met during his journey?

2. What was Steinbeck's opinion of super-highways?

SHORT ANSWER UNIT TEST 1 *Travels With Charley* Page 2

3. What was considered the great get-together symbol on the highways?

4. What questions did Steinbeck have about Americans and roots?

5. Redwoods were once located in England, Europe and America. What happened to them?

6. Which state is the only state that came into the Union in a treaty?

SHORT ANSWER UNIT TEST 1 *Travels With Charley* Page 3

7. Why did Steinbeck dread traveling to the South?

8. Who were the Cheerleaders?

9. How did Steinbeck wash his clothes while he was traveling?

10. What did Steinbeck think was happening to regional speech?

SHORT ANSWER UNIT TEST 1 *Travels With Charley* Page 4

<u>III. Essay</u>

Prior to the beginning of his journey, Steinbeck felt that a journey was a person in itself and that "we do not take a trip; a trip takes us." Was this true for Steinbeck's own journey across America? Explain in detail why or why not.

SHORT ANSWER UNIT TEST 1 *Travels With Charley* Page 5

IV. Vocabulary

Directions: Listen to the vocabulary word and spell it. After you have spelled all the words, go back and write down the definitions.

WORD   DEFINITION

1. _____   _____
2. _____   _____
3. _____   _____
4. _____   _____
5. _____   _____
6. _____   _____
7. _____   _____
8. _____   _____
9. _____   _____
10. _____   _____

ANSWER KEY: SHORT ANSWER UNIT TEST 1 *Travels With Charley*

1. Matching/Identification

I 1. Rocinante   A. work of an evil child
G 2. Charley   B. reminder of Avalon
J 3. Fayre Eleyne   C. wife visited author here
A 4. Bad Lands   D. author's birthplace
B 5. Deer Isle   E. journey's beginning
E 6. Sag Harbor   F. a state of mind
H 7. Mojave Desert   G. dog
F 8. Texas   H. forced the will to survive
C 9. Chicago   I. truck
D 10. Salinas   J. boat

II. Short Answer

1. What did Steinbeck see in the eyes of many of the people he met during his journey?
    He saw a look of longing. People wished to be able to do what he was doing.

2. What was Steinbeck's opinion of super-highways?
    He thought that they were wonderful for moving goods, but that they were not very good for people who were interested in seeing the countryside of America.

3. What was considered the great get-together symbol on the highways?
    A cup of coffee was the symbol.

4. What questions did Steinbeck have about Americans and roots?
    Are Americans restless and never satisfied? Is the need or urge to be somewhere else greater than the need for roots?

5. Redwoods were once located in England, Europe and America. What happened to them?
    They were wiped out by the moving glaciers.

6. Which state is the only state that came into the Union in a treaty?
    Texas is the only one.

7. Why did Steinbeck dread traveling to the South?
   He knew he would see pain, fear, bewilderment and confusion caused by desegregation.

8. Who were the Cheerleaders?
   They were a group of white women who would gather at the school to scream at the black students.

9. How did Steinbeck wash his clothes while he was traveling?
   He placed the clothes, soap, and water into a garbage bucket tied to the closet pole in the back of his truck. The truck's movement juggled the contents for the entire driving day. He rinsed the clothes at the end of the day, and dried them the next day on a line in the truck.

10. What did Steinbeck think was happening to regional speech?
    He thought that regional speech was perhaps disappearing because people were listening to radio and television voices so much.

III. Essay Answers will depend on your class discussions. Grade these on your own criteria.

IV. Vocabulary: Choose ten of the vocabulary words to dictate for this section of the test.

WORD	DEFINITION
1. _____	_____
2. _____	_____
3. _____	_____
4. _____	_____
5. _____	_____
6. _____	_____
7. _____	_____
8. _____	_____
9. _____	_____
10. _____	_____

SHORT ANSWER UNIT TEST 2 *Travels With Charley*

I. Matching/Identification

_____1. Amarillo   A. sculptured by Ice Age

_____2. Chicago   B. east-west middle of the country

_____3. Wisconsin Dells   C. Steinbeck's birthplace

_____4. Fargo, North Dakota   D. starting point for trip

_____5. Montana   E. Steinbeck was not objective about this area

_____6. Salinas, California   F. Charley was left there for a while

_____7. Sag harbor, New York   G. actual ending point of trip

_____8. Abingdon, Virginia   H. Steinbeck went there to witness desegregation

_____9. Texas   I. Steinbeck's wife met him there

_____10. New Orleans   J. Steinbeck fell in love with this area

II. Short Answer

1. Where in the country did Steinbeck believe the east-west middle should be?

2. Where did Steinbeck like to observe people?

SHORT ANSWER UNIT TEST 2 *Travels With Charley* Page 2

3. Why did Steinbeck consider mobile homes to be a revolution in living?

4. What did Steinbeck learn about Charley at Yellowstone?

5. Why did Steinbeck dread traveling to the South?

6. What was the final event of Steinbeck's journey?

SHORT ANSWER UNIT TEST 2 *Travels With Charley* Page 3

7. What factor found in all living things was especially present in the desert?

8. On what issue did Steinbeck and his sisters argue constantly?

9. What tree causes wonder and respect in men?

10. What did Steinbeck tell Robbie's father about hairdressers?

SHORT ANSWER UNIT TEST 2 *Travels With Charley* Page 4

III. Essay

Describe the end of Steinbeck's trip. Tell where he said he was when he knew the trip was over. Summarize his thoughts and actions for the remainder of the trip.

SHORT ANSWER UNIT TEST 2 *Travels With Charley* Page 5

IV. Vocabulary

Directions: Listen to the vocabulary word and spell it. After you have spelled all the words, go back and write down the definitions.

WORD	DEFINITION
1. _____	_____
2. _____	_____
3. _____	_____
4. _____	_____
5. _____	_____
6. _____	_____
7. _____	_____
8. _____	_____
9. _____	_____
10. _____	_____

ANSWER KEY: SHORT ANSWER UNIT TEST 2 *Travels With Charley*

1. Matching/Identification

F. 1. Amarillo A. sculptured by Ice Age
I. 2. Chicago B. east-west middle of the country
A. 3. Wisconsin Dells C. Steinbeck's birthplace
B. 4. Fargo, North Dakota D. starting point for trip
J. 5. Montana E. Steinbeck was not objective about this area
C. 6. Salinas, California F. Charley was left there for a while
D. 7. Sag Harbor, New York G. actual ending point of trip
G. 8. Abingdon, Virginia H. Steinbeck went there to witness desegregation
E. 9. Texas I. Steinbeck's wife met him there
H. 10. New Orleans J. Steinbeck fell in love with this area

II. Short Answer

1. Where in the country did Steinbeck believe the east-west middle should be?
    He thought it should be at the Missouri River at Bismarck, North Dakota.

2. Where did Steinbeck like to observe people?
    He went to bars, churches and roadside restaurants. He also listened to the morning radio.

3. Why did Steinbeck consider mobile homes to be a revolution in living?
    He thought they were comfortable, compact, easy to keep clean, and easy to heat.

4. What did Steinbeck learn about Charley at Yellowstone?
    He found out that Charley was not as peace-loving and cowardly as he had believed. Charley wanted to fight the bears!

5. Why did Steinbeck dread traveling to the South?
    He knew he would see pain, fear, bewilderment and confusion caused by desegregation.

6. What was the final event of Steinbeck's journey?
    He got lost in his own hometown.

7. What factor found in all living things was especially present in the desert?
    The will and need to survive was especially strong in the desert life.

8. On what issue did Steinbeck and his sisters argue constantly?
    They argued about politics.

9. What tree causes wonder and respect in men?
    The giant redwood trees do.

10. What did Steinbeck tell Robbie's father about hairdressers?
   He told him that women confided in their hairdressers and that gave the hairdressers a lot of power.

III. Essay

Describe the end of Steinbeck's trip. Tell where he said he was when he knew the trip was over. Summarize his thoughts and actions for the remainder of the trip.

Answers will depend on your class discussions. Grade these on your own criteria.

IV. Vocabulary: Choose ten of the vocabulary words to dictate for this section of the test.

WORD	DEFINITION
1. _____	_____
2. _____	_____
3. _____	_____
4. _____	_____
5. _____	_____
6. _____	_____
7. _____	_____
8. _____	_____
9. _____	_____
10. _____	_____

ADVANCED SHORT ANSWER UNIT TEST *Travels With Charley*

I. Matching/Identification

____1. Amarillo   A. sculptured by Ice Age
____2. Chicago   B. east-west middle of the country
____3. Wisconsin Dells   C. Steinbeck's birthplace
____4. Fargo, North Dakota   D. starting point for trip
____5. Montana   E. Steinbeck was not objective about this area
____6. Salinas, California   F. Charley was left there for a while
____7. Sag harbor, New York   G. actual ending point of trip
____8. Abingdon, Virginia   H. Steinbeck went there to witness desegregation
____9. Texas   I. Steinbeck's wife met him there
____10. New Orleans   J. Steinbeck fell in love with this area

II. Short Answer

1. Prior to the beginning of his journey, Steinbeck felt that a journey was a person in itself and that "we do not take a trip; a trip takes us." Was this true for Steinbeck's own journey across America? Explain in detail why or why not.

2. Why did Steinbeck dread traveling to the South? Describe in detail what he found there. Include the incident with the Cheerleaders.

ADVANCED SHORT ANSWER UNIT TEST *Travels With Charley* Page 2

3. Describe Steinbeck's trip through Yellowstone National Park. Include the new information he learned about Charley.

4. What questions did Steinbeck have about Americans and roots? What, if any, answers did he find?

5. Discuss the end of the trip. Where did Steinbeck say the trip actually ended before he returned home? What happened when he reached the Holland Tunnel? What was the final event of Steinbeck's journey?

ADVANCED SHORT ANSWER UNIT TEST *Travels With Charley* Page 3

III. Essay

So, in essence, what did Steinbeck find out about America and Americans on his trip?

ADVANCED SHORT ANSWER UNIT TEST *Travels With Charley* Page 4

IV. Vocabulary

Directions: Listen to the words and write them down. After you have written down all of the words, write a paragraph in which you use all of the words. The paragraph must relate in some way to the book *Travels With Charley*.

MULTIPLE CHOICE UNIT TEST 1 *Travels With Charley*

I. Matching/Identification:

1. Amarillo   A. sculptured by Ice Age
2. Chicago   B. east-west middle of the country
3. Wisconsin Dells   C. Steinbeck's birthplace
4. Fargo, North Dakota   D. starting point for trip
5. Montana   E. Steinbeck was not objective about this area
6. Salinas, California   F. Charley was left there for a while
7. Sag Harbor, New York   G. actual ending point of trip
8. Abingdon, Virginia   H. Steinbeck went there to witness desegregation
9. Texas   I. Steinbeck's wife met him there
10. New Orleans   J. Steinbeck fell in love with this area

II. Multiple Choice
1. Describe the type of vehicle Steinbeck required for his journey.
    A. He needed a 6-cylinder mini-van with a tow bar.
    B. He needed a station wagon with air conditioning.
    C. He needed a motorcycle with a sidecar.
    D. He needed a four-wheel drive, 3/4-ton pick-up truck with a camper top.

2. What did Steinbeck name his vehicle?
    A. Rocinante
    B. Betelgeuse
    C. Road Warrior
    D. Gulliver

3. Who was Charley?
    A. He was a Siamese cat.
    B. He was a french poodle.
    C. He was Steinbeck's son.
    D. He was Steinbeck's brother.

4. True or False: Steinbeck saw a look of longing in the eyes of many of the people he met during his journey. People wished to be able to do what he was doing.
    A. True
    B. False

MULTIPLE CHOICE UNIT TEST 1 *Travels With Charley* Page 2

5. What word means, "the act of going somewhere with a direction in mind but not caring whether or not you get there"?
    A. migrating
    B. vacilado
    C. sashay
    D. promenade

6. What was Steinbeck talking about? He thought that they were wonderful for moving goods, but that they were not very good for people who were interested in seeing the countryside of America.
    A. moving vans
    B. trains
    C. super-highways
    D. airplanes

7. Steinbeck thought that _____ was perhaps disappearing because people were listening to radio and television voices so much.
    A. good grammar
    B. the art of public speaking
    C. regional speech
    D. conversation between friends

8. Steinbeck told Robbie's father that women confided in their _____ and that gave those people a lot of power.
    A. priests
    B. hairdressers
    C. appliance repairmen
    D. husbands

9. On what issue did Steinbeck and his sisters argue constantly?
    A. They argued about family history.
    B. They argued about money.
    C. They argued about politics.
    D. They argued about food.

10. True or False: By the time he got to his last stop, Steinbeck was ready to start all over on another trip.
    A. True
    B. False

MULTIPLE CHOICE UNIT TEST 1 *Travels With Charley* Page 3

III. Vocabulary Directions: Match the word and its meaning.

___ 1. ENVOY   A. Lament; feel or express deep sorrow

___ 2. VAGUELY   B. Gaudy & cheap

___ 3. APHIDS   C. Not clearly expressed or defined

___ 4. POSTULATE   D. Skilled; perfect

___ 5. CORROBORATE   E. Abusive, insulting expressions

___ 6. DEPLORE   F. Attested to the truth or accuracy of something

___ 7. COERCION   G. Highest point; culmination

___ 8. TAWDRY   H. Messenger

___ 9. DAWDLE   I. Terse; concise; succinct

___ 10. PERNICIOUS   J. Small soft-bodied insects that suck sap from plants

___ 11. INVECTIVES   K. Can't be corrected or reformed

___ 12. APEX   L. Statement generally accepted without proof

___ 13. KIN   M. Relatives

___ 14. ANARCHISM   N. Forcing to think or act in a certain manner by threat or force

___ 15. OBSOLESCENCE O. Destructive; harmful

___ 16. PISCINE   P. Wasting time lingering

___ 17. ELATE   Q. Theory that all governments are bad & should be abolished

___ 18. INCORRIGIBLE R. Relating to fish

___ 19. LACONIC   S. Raise the spirits of; make joyful

___ 20. CONSUMMATE   T. Being replaced by something newer

ANSWER SHEET MULTIPLE CHOICE UNIT TEST 1 *Travels with Charley*

	Matching	Multiple Choice	Vocabulary
1			
2			
3			
4			
5			
6			
7			
8			
9			
10			
11	xxxx	xxxx	
12	xxxx	xxxx	
13	xxxx	xxxx	
14	xxxx	xxxx	
15	xxxx	xxxx	
16	xxxx	xxxx	
17	xxxx	xxxx	
18	xxxx	xxxx	
19	xxxx	xxxx	
20	xxxx	xxxx	

ANSWER SHEET KEY MULTIPLE CHOICE UNIT TEST 1 *Travels with Charley*

	Matching	Multiple Choice	Vocabulary
1	F	D	H
2	I	A	C
3	A	B	J
4	B	A	L
5	J	B	F
6	C	C	A
7	D	C	N
8	G	B	B
9	E	C	P
10	H	B	O
11	xxxx	xxxx	E
12	xxxx	xxxx	G
13	xxxx	xxxx	M
14	xxxx	xxxx	Q
15	xxxx	xxxx	T
16	xxxx	xxxx	R
17	xxxx	xxxx	S
18	xxxx	xxxx	K
19	xxxx	xxxx	I
20	xxxx	xxxx	D

MULTIPLE CHOICE UNIT TEST 2 *Travels with Charley*

I. Matching/Identification

_____ 1. Rocinante   A. work of an evil child

_____ 2. Charley   B. reminder of Avalon

_____ 3. Fayre Eleyne   C. wife visited author here

_____ 4. Bad Lands   D. author's birthplace

_____ 5. Deer Isle   E. journey's beginning

_____ 6. Sag Harbor   F. a state of mind

_____ 7. Mojave Desert   G. dog

_____ 8. Texas   H. forced the will to survive

_____ 9. Chicago   I. truck

_____ 10. Salinas   J. boat

II. Multiple Choice

1. Where in the country did Steinbeck believe the east-west middle of the country should be?
    A. at the Continental Divide in Colorado
    B. at the Grand Canyon
    C. at the Missouri River at Bismarck, North Dakota
    D. at the Mississippi River in St. Louis, Missouri

2. Where did Steinbeck like to observe people?
    A. He went to schools, bookstores, and concert halls.
    B. He went to libraries, department stores, and hospitals.
    C. He went to grocery stores, parks, and bus stations.
    D. He went to bars, churches and roadside restaurants.

3. What is Steinbeck taking about? He thought they were a revolution in living. He thought they were comfortable, compact, easy to keep clean, and easy to heat.
    A. mobile homes
    B. minivans
    C. passenger trains
    D. commuter airplanes

4. What did Charley want to do at Yellowstone?
    A. Charley wanted to swim in the water of Old Faithful.
    B. Charley wanted to play with the children he met.
    C. Charley wanted to fight the bears!
    D. Charley wanted to chase squirrels.

MULTIPLE CHOICE UNIT TEST 2 *Travels with Charley* Page 2

5. Steinbeck dreaded traveling to the South because he knew he would see pain, fear, bewilderment and confusion caused by _____.
    A. poverty
    B. war
    C. desegregation
    D. religion

6. What was the final event of Steinbeck's journey?
    A. Someone stole the truck from his driveway.
    B. The town had a parade for him.
    C. He got lost in his own hometown.
    D. Charley died.

7. What factor found in all living things was especially present in the desert?
    A. It was the will and need to survive.
    B. It was a fierce sense of competition.
    C. It was a spirit of cooperation.
    D. It was a relaxed attitude about life.

8. On what issue did Steinbeck and his sisters argue constantly?
    A. They argued about politics.
    B. They argued about money.
    C. They argued about family history.
    D. They argued about food.

9. What tree causes wonder and respect in men?
    A. The live oak tree.
    B. The bonsai tree.
    C. The palm tree.
    D. The giant redwood tree.

10. Steinbeck told Robbie's father that women confided in their _____ and that gave those people a lot of power.
    A. ministers
    B. hairdressers
    C. appliance repairmen
    D. husbands

MULTIPLE CHOICE UNIT TEST 2 *Travels with Charley*

III. Vocabulary

____ 1. COURTEOUS   A. Forcing to think or act in a certain manner by threat or force

____ 2. ENVOY   B. Expressing much in a few words

____ 3. DEPLORE   C. Lament; feel or express deep sorrow

____ 4. ORGY   D. Relating to fish

____ 5. INCORRIGIBLE   E. Statement on which an argument is based or from which a conclusion is drawn

____ 6. TAWDRY   F. Gaudy & cheap

____ 7. LACONIC   G. To obtain forcefully

____ 8. PISCINE   H. Showiness to impress others

____ 9. DEBRIS   I. Anyone especially cruel, brutish, or hideous

____ 10. PREMISE   J. A revel involving unrestrained indulgence

____ 11. COERCION   K. Classic; characterized by enduring appeal

____ 12. OSTENTATION   L. Terse; concise; succinct

____ 13. OGRE   M. Pertaining to the sense of beauty

____ 14. WREST   N. Attested to the truth or accuracy of something

____ 15. VICARIOUS   O. Messenger

____ 16. VINTAGE   P. Scattered remains of something broken

____ 17. KIN   Q. Polite

____ 18. CORROBORATE   R. Experienced through imaginative participation in the experiences of others

____ 19. AESTHETIC   S. Relatives

____ 20. CONCISE   T. Can't be corrected or reformed

ANSWER SHEET MULTIPLE CHOICE UNIT TEST 2 *Travels with Charley*

	Matching	Multiple Choice	Vocabulary
1			
2			
3			
4			
5			
6			
7			
8			
9			
10			
11	xxxx	xxxx	
12	xxxx	xxxx	
13	xxxx	xxxx	
14	xxxx	xxxx	
15	xxxx	xxxx	
16	xxxx	xxxx	
17	xxxx	xxxx	
18	xxxx	xxxx	
19	xxxx	xxxx	
20	xxxx	xxxx	

ANSWER SHEET KEY MULTIPLE CHOICE UNIT TEST 2 *Travels with Charley*

	Matching	Multiple Choice	Vocabulary
1	I	C	Q
2	G	D	O
3	J	A	C
4	A	C	J
5	B	C	T
6	E	C	F
7	H	A	L
8	F	A	D
9	C	D	P
10	D	B	E
11	xxxx	xxxx	A
12	xxxx	xxxx	H
13	xxxx	xxxx	I
14	xxxx	xxxx	G
15	xxxx	xxxx	R
16	xxxx	xxxx	K
17	xxxx	xxxx	S
18	xxxx	xxxx	N
19	xxxx	xxxx	M
20	xxxx	xxxx	B

UNIT RESOURCE MATERIALS

BULLETIN BOARD IDEAS - *Travels With Charley*

1. Save one corner of the board for the best of students' Travels With Charley writing assignments.

2. Take one of the word search puzzles from the extra activities packet and (with a marker) copy it over in a large size on the bulletin board. Write the clue words to one side. Invite students prior to and after class to find the words and circle them on the bulletin board.

3. See the introductory activity, Lesson One.

4. Post a map of the U.S. and trace Steinbeck's journey (as well as can be done) with a red marker.

5. Steinbeck's journey covered the areas of New England, mid-west, pacific northwest, southwest, and south. Display maps, pictures showing the different landscapes, cultures, foods, and agriculture, etc. from each region.

6. Place a map of the U.S. on the bulletin board and have students mark with a red X the places they have been. (This works really well if your school is near a military base or if you are in an affluent area where parents take kids on a lot of great vacations.)

7. Title the board AMERICANS ON THE MOVE. Post information & pictures about the restless nature of Americans, beginning with the early pioneers.

8. Do a bulletin board about issues facing our cities.

9. Do a bulletin board about careers related to the travel industry.

EXTRA ACTIVITIES - *Travels With Charley*

One of the difficulties in teaching a novel is that all students don't read at the same speed. One student who likes to read may take the book home and finish it in a day or two. Sometimes a few students finish the in-class assignments early. The problem, then, is finding suitable extra activities for students.

One thing that seems to help is to keep a little library in the classroom. For this unit on *Travels With Charley*, you might check out from the school library other novels and stories by Steinbeck. A biography or articles about the author would be interesting for some students. You can include other related books and articles about travel, points of interest in the country, issues facing cities and towns in this decade, and the issues in the U.S. at the time Steinbeck took his trip (desegregation, for example). Articles of criticism about Steinbeck's works might also provide some interesting reading for some students.

Other things you may keep on hand are puzzles. We have made some relating directly to *Travels With Charley* for you. Feel free to duplicate them for your students to use.

Some students may like to draw. You might devise a contest or allow some extra-credit grade for students who draw characters or scenes from *Travels With Charley*. Note, too, that if the students do not want to keep their drawings you may pick up some extra bulletin board materials this way. If you have a contest and you supply the prize (a CD or something like that perhaps), you could, possibly, make the drawing itself a non-returnable entry fee.

The pages which follow contain games, puzzles and worksheets. The keys, when appropriate, immediately follow the puzzle or worksheet. There are two main groups of activities: one group for the unit; that is, generally relating to *Travels With Charley* text, and another group of activities related strictly to *Travels With Charley* vocabulary.

Directions for these games, puzzles and worksheets are self-explanatory. The object here is to provide you with extra materials you may use in any way you choose.

MORE ACTIVITIES - *Travels With Charley*

1. Have students design a book cover (front and back and inside flaps) for *Travels With Charley*.

2. Have students design a bulletin board (ready to be put up; not just sketched) for *Travels With Charley*.

3. Play a word-association game. Name a city or a place people sometimes visit. Ask students what comes to mind when they hear that place mentioned. See what pre-conceived notions people have about places they have not visited.

4. Use some of the related topics (noted earlier for an in-class library) as topics for research, reports or written papers, or as topics for guest speakers.

5. Research what careers are currently available in the travel industry.

6. Have students make a travelogue for your hometown. They could do a video, make brochures, take pictures of the highlights of your town, etc.

7. Have students take a survey of people in your school or community to determine where the most popular vacation places are.

8. Have students write a letter from Steinbeck to his wife in Steinbeck's writing style.

9. Invite a long-distance trucker in to talk about his work and life on the road.

10. Have a banquet for which each student prepares a dish from some region of the U.S. (Examples: chili from the southwest, New England pot roast, southern fried chicken, an apple dish from Washington state, a salad using Florida or California oranges, etc.)

11. Spend some time talking about American speech. Discuss regional expressions and accents.

12. Have students work together to make a time line chronology of the events in the story. Take a large piece of construction paper and on one wall (or however you can physically arrange it in your room) and make the events of the story along it. Students may want to add drawings or cut-out pictures to represent the events (as well as a written statement).

Travels With Charley Word List

No.	Word	Clue/Definition
1.	CHICAGO	Place where Mr. Steinbeck's wife met him to visit
2.	CANUCKS	Maine's migrant farmers
3.	MONTANA	State Mr. Steinbeck considered a great splash of grandeur
4.	FIRE	Kind of sermon in Vermont: ___ & Brimstone
5.	GLACIERS	Responsible for wiping out most of the redwood trees
6.	RABIES	Charley didn't have his certificate of vaccination for this
7.	CHARLEY	The poodle; companion to Mr. Steinbeck
8.	QUIXOTE	Rocinante was named for Don ___'s horse
9.	COFFEE	It is the great get-together symbol
10.	CHEERLEADERS	Group of white women gathered at school to protest desegregation
11.	TWIN	Minneapolis & St. Paul are the ___ Cities
12.	FARGO	The east-west middle of the country was in ___, ND
13.	VIRGINIA	In this state Mr. Steinbeck realized his trip had ended
14.	CHILD	The Bad Lands seemed like the work of an evil ___
15.	MISSOURI	This river, according to Mr. Steinbeck, should have been the east-west middle of the country
16.	ROCINANTE	The truck
17.	TRUTH	Near the end of the book, Mr. Steinbeck gave reasons why he couldn't find the ___ about the country
18.	THOUGHT	A man has to have feelings and then words before he can come close to this
19.	HARBOR	Sag ___; starting point of the trip
20.	REDWOOD	These trees cause wonder & respect in man
21.	ORLEANS	New ___; place where the Cheerleaders demonstrated
22.	VACILANDO	Going somewhere with a direction in mind but not caring if you get there or not
23.	WIFE	The boat was named for Steinbeck's
24.	CANADA	This country wouldn't let Charley in
25.	DELLS	Wisconsin ___; formed by ice during the Ice Age
26.	MOBILE	These homes were revolutionary
27.	ELEYNE	Fair ___; the boat
28.	TEXAS	Only state to enter the union by treaty
29.	AMBASSADOR	Hotel in Chicago: ___ East
30.	POLITICS	Topic of family arguments
31.	TRIP	You don't take one, one takes you
32.	ROBBIE	He wanted to be a hairdresser
33.	TRAVELS	___ With Charley
34.	POTATO	Mr. Steinbeck wanted to see these crops in Maine
35.	MOJAVE	Desert Mr. Steinbeck and Charley crossed
36.	AVALON	Deer Isle was like ___
37.	ALLERGIC	Charley was ___ to insecticides
38.	TRUCKERS	They have their own language, according to Mr. Steinbeck
39.	ICEBREAKER	Mr. Steinbeck used Charley as this with strangers
40.	HARRY	Lonesome ___; previous occupant of the hotel room
41.	BEARS	Charley wanted to fight them at Yellowstone
42.	MAINE	White Mountains are in this state
43.	STEINBECK	Author
44.	MIND	Texas is a state of ___, according to Mr. Steinbeck

Travels With Charley Word List Continured

No.	Word	Clue/Definition
45.	SALINAS	Mr. Steinbeck's home town in California
46.	COYOTES	Two cans of dog food were left for them

Travels With Charley Word Search

```
S A L I N A S S C H I C A G O Q N W
D O O W D E R N H A R O Y Q D R M
L V E M T A E A A P R O F W K L C
B J N O E R D E R O P A R B F T D M
T Z Y B M P A L L L R V D Y B E T B
K O E I F L E R E I O W L A L I E Y
C C L L J L L O Y T C H T L P Q E G
C P E E D S R G X I I L S X W W L Y
Q U I X O T E D R C N M S N R A V R
M O J A V E E C O S A H A D C A A D
C J T F Y I H Z B S N T M I Y L C N
R H W H T N C T R Q T U E V N L I V
A H I C E B R E A K E R W I F E L M
B Y N L T E K K H W S T I A I R A M
I X R D D C A N U C K S R P R G N L
E G N W U K N T H O U G H T E I D N
S I Q R T E X A S N O L A V A C O P
M B T R A V E L S P O T A T O S M V
```

ALLERGIC	COFFEE	ICEBREAKER	RABIES	TRIP
AVALON	COYOTES	MAINE	REDWOOD	TRUCKERS
BEARS	DELLS	MIND	ROBBIE	TRUTH
CANADA	ELEYNE	MOBILE	ROCINANTE	TWIN
CANUCKS	FARGO	MOJAVE	SALINAS	VACILANDO
CHARLEY	FIRE	ORLEANS	STEINBECK	WIFE
CHEERLEADERS	GLACIERS	POLITICS	TEXAS	
CHICAGO	HARBOR	POTATO	THOUGHT	
CHILD	HARRY	QUIXOTE	TRAVELS	

Travels With Charley Word Search Answer Key

```
S A L I N A S S C H I C A G O
D O O W D E R N H A A R O
    E M T A E A P N R O F
    N O E   D E R O   A R B F   D
    Y B     A L L R   D Y B E
  O E I     A E I O     A L I E
C   L L     E R T C     L   E G
    E E   S R O Y I   S     A V
Q U I X O T E     R C N M     A V
M O J A V E E     O S A   C   A C
C     T   I H     B S T I     L I
R H W     N C     R   U E   N L L
A   I C E B R E A K E R W I F E L
B   N L   E K     H   S I A   R A
I     D D C A N U C K S R P R G N
E   N   U K   T H O U G H T E I D
S I     R T E X A S N O L A V A C
M   T R A V E L S P O T A T O
```

ALLERGIC	COFFEE	ICEBREAKER	RABIES	TRIP
AVALON	COYOTES	MAINE	REDWOOD	TRUCKERS
BEARS	DELLS	MIND	ROBBIE	TRUTH
CANADA	ELEYNE	MOBILE	ROCINANTE	TWIN
CANUCKS	FARGO	MOJAVE	SALINAS	VACILANDO
CHARLEY	FIRE	ORLEANS	STEINBECK	WIFE
CHEERLEADERS	GLACIERS	POLITICS	TEXAS	
CHICAGO	HARBOR	POTATO	THOUGHT	
CHILD	HARRY	QUIXOTE	TRAVELS	

Travels With Charley Crossword

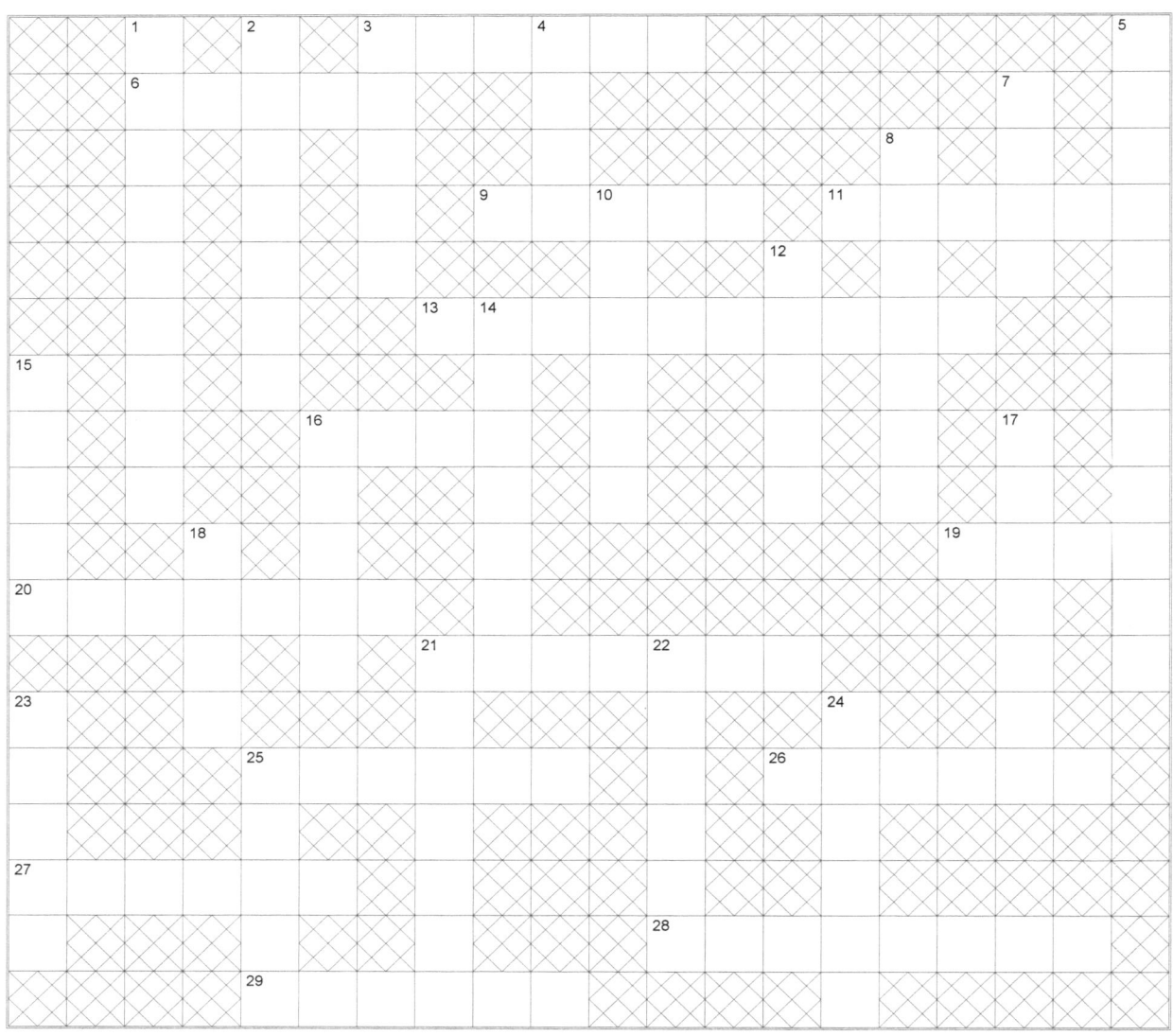

Across

3. It is the great get-together symbol
6. Near the end of the book, Mr. Steinbeck gave reasons why he couldn't find the ___ about the country
9. Charley wanted to fight them at Yellowstone
11. These homes were revolutionary
13. Hotel in Chicago: ___ East
16. Minneapolis & St. Paul are the ___ Cities
19. The boat was named for Steinbeck's ___
20. Mr. Steinbeck's home town in California
21. Maine's migrant farmers
25. Desert Mr. Steinbeck and Charley crossed
26. Sag ___; starting point of the trip
27. He wanted to be a hairdresser
28. Charley was ___ to insecticides
29. Fair ___; the boat

Down

1. Author
2. Rocinante was named for Don ___'s horse
3. The Bad Lands seemed like the work of an evil ___
4. Kind of sermon in Vermont: ___ & Brimstone
5. Group of white women gathered at school to protest desegregation
7. You don't take one, one takes you
8. Two cans of dog food were left for them
10. Deer Isle was like ___
12. The east-west middle of the country was in ___, ND
14. State Mr. Steinbeck considered a great splash of grandeur
15. Wisconsin ___; formed by ice during the Ice Age
16. Only state to enter the union by treaty
17. Place where Mr. Steinbeck's wife met him to visit
18. Texas is a state of ___, according to Mr. Steinbeck
21. The poodle; companion to Mr. Steinbeck
22. This country wouldn't let Charley in
23. Lonesome ___; previous occupant of the hotel room
24. Charley didn't have his certificate of vaccination for this
25. White Mountains are in this state

Travels With Charley Crossword Answer Key

		1 S		2 Q		3 C	O	4 F	F	E	E				5 C
		6 T	R	U	T	H		I					7 T		H
		E		I		I		R			8 C		R		E
		I		X		L		9 B	10 E	A	R	S	11 M	O	B	I	L	E
		N		O		D			V		12 F	Y		P		R
		B		T		13 A	14 M	B	A	S	S	A	D	O	R		L
15 D		E		E			O		L		R		T			E
E		C		16 T	W	I	N		O		G		E		17 C		A
L		K		E			T		N		O		S		H		D
L		18 M		X			A						19 W	I	F	E
20 S	A	L	I	N	A	S		N						C		R
		N		S		21 C	A	N	U	22 C	K	S			A		S
23 H		D				H				A			24 R		G	
A				25 M	O	J	A	V	E		N		26 H	A	R	B	O	R
R				A		A			R			A		B		
27 R	O	B	B	I	E		L			D		I			
Y				N			E		28 A	L	L	E	R	G	I	C
				29 E	L	E	Y	N	E			S			

Across
3. It is the great get-together symbol
6. Near the end of the book, Mr. Steinbeck gave reasons why he couldn't find the ___ about the country
9. Charley wanted to fight them at Yellowstone
11. These homes were revolutionary
13. Hotel in Chicago: ___ East
16. Minneapolis & St. Paul are the ___ Cities
19. The boat was named for Steinbeck's
20. Mr. Steinbeck's home town in California
21. Maine's migrant farmers
25. Desert Mr. Steinbeck and Charley crossed
26. Sag ___; starting point of the trip
27. He wanted to be a hairdresser
28. Charley was ___ to insecticides
29. Fair ___; the boat

Down
1. Author
2. Rocinante was named for Don ___'s horse
3. The Bad Lands seemed like the work of an evil ____
4. Kind of sermon in Vermont: ___ & Brimstone
5. Group of white women gathered at school to protest desegregation
7. You don't take one, one takes you
8. Two cans of dog food were left for them
10. Deer Isle was like ____
12. The east-west middle of the country was in ___, ND
14. State Mr. Steinbeck considered a great splash of grandeur
15. Wisconsin ___; formed by ice during the Ice Age
16. Only state to enter the union by treaty
17. Place where Mr. Steinbeck's wife met him to visit
18. Texas is a state of ____, according to Mr. Steinbeck
21. The poodle; companion to Mr. Steinbeck
22. This country wouldn't let Charley in
23. Lonesome ___; previous occupant of the hotel room
24. Charley didn't have his certificate of vaccination for this
25. White Mountains are in this state

Travels With Charley Matching Worksheet 1

___ 1. HARRY   A. Maine's migrant farmers
___ 2. SALINAS   B. White Mountains are in this state
___ 3. WIFE   C. Responsible for wiping out most of the redwood trees
___ 4. FARGO   D. The boat was named for Steinbeck's
___ 5. MISSOURI   E. Author
___ 6. CANUCKS   F. This river, according to Mr. Steinbeck, should have been the east-west middle of the country
___ 7. REDWOOD   G. You don't take one, one takes you
___ 8. ROCINANTE   H. Hotel in Chicago: ___ East
___ 9. THOUGHT   I. It is the great get-together symbol
___10. COFFEE   J. A man has to have feelings and then words before he can come close to this
___11. CHARLEY   K. Going somewhere with a direction in mind but not caring if you get there or not
___12. STEINBECK   L. The east-west middle of the country was in ___, ND
___13. VIRGINIA   M. Mr. Steinbeck's home town in California
___14. BEARS   N. Rocinante was named for Don ___'s horse
___15. CHILD   O. In this state Mr. Steinbeck realized his trip had ended
___16. DELLS   P. The Bad Lands seemed like the work of an evil ___
___17. QUIXOTE   Q. Charley wanted to fight them at Yellowstone
___18. ELEYNE   R. The poodle; companion to Mr. Steinbeck
___19. GLACIERS   S. Wisconsin ___; formed by ice during the Ice Age
___20. MAINE   T. Fair ___; the boat
___21. VACILANDO   U. Texas is a state of ____, according to Mr. Steinbeck
___22. TRIP   V. Minneapolis & St. Paul are the ___ Cities
___23. AMBASSADOR   W. These trees cause wonder & respect in man
___24. TWIN   X. The truck
___25. MIND   Y. Lonesome ___; previous occupant of the hotel room

Travels With Charley Matching Worksheet 1 Answer Key

Y - 1.	HARRY	A.	Maine's migrant farmers
M - 2.	SALINAS	B.	White Mountains are in this state
D - 3.	WIFE	C.	Responsible for wiping out most of the redwood trees
L - 4.	FARGO	D.	The boat was named for Steinbeck's
F - 5.	MISSOURI	E.	Author
A - 6.	CANUCKS	F.	This river, according to Mr. Steinbeck, should have been the east-west middle of the country
W - 7.	REDWOOD	G.	You don't take one, one takes you
X - 8.	ROCINANTE	H.	Hotel in Chicago: ___ East
J - 9.	THOUGHT	I.	It is the great get-together symbol
I - 10.	COFFEE	J.	A man has to have feelings and then words before he can come close to this
R - 11.	CHARLEY	K.	Going somewhere with a direction in mind but not caring if you get there or not
E - 12.	STEINBECK	L.	The east-west middle of the country was in ___, ND
O - 13.	VIRGINIA	M.	Mr. Steinbeck's home town in California
Q - 14.	BEARS	N.	Rocinante was named for Don ___'s horse
P - 15.	CHILD	O.	In this state Mr. Steinbeck realized his trip had ended
S - 16.	DELLS	P.	The Bad Lands seemed like the work of an evil ___
N - 17.	QUIXOTE	Q.	Charley wanted to fight them at Yellowstone
T - 18.	ELEYNE	R.	The poodle; companion to Mr. Steinbeck
C - 19.	GLACIERS	S.	Wisconsin ___; formed by ice during the Ice Age
B - 20.	MAINE	T.	Fair ___; the boat
K - 21.	VACILANDO	U.	Texas is a state of ____, according to Mr. Steinbeck
G - 22.	TRIP	V.	Minneapolis & St. Paul are the ___ Cities
H - 23.	AMBASSADOR	W.	These trees cause wonder & respect in man
V - 24.	TWIN	X.	The truck
U - 25.	MIND	Y.	Lonesome ___; previous occupant of the hotel room

Travels With Charley Matching Worksheet 2

___ 1. ROCINANTE   A. Charley was ___ to insecticides
___ 2. STEINBECK   B. White Mountains are in this state
___ 3. MAINE   C. He wanted to be a hairdresser
___ 4. ICEBREAKER   D. ____ With Charley
___ 5. TRAVELS   E. Topic of family arguments
___ 6. COYOTES   F. Lonesome ___; previous occupant of the hotel room
___ 7. ALLERGIC   G. Near the end of the book, Mr. Steinbeck gave reasons why he couldn't find the ___ about the country
___ 8. COFFEE   H. Maine's migrant farmers
___ 9. FIRE   I. Going somewhere with a direction in mind but not caring if you get there or not
___10. HARBOR   J. Rocinante was named for Don ___'s horse
___11. VACILANDO   K. The Bad Lands seemed like the work of an evil ____
___12. CANADA   L. Mr. Steinbeck used Charley as this with strangers
___13. ELEYNE   M. Deer Isle was like ____
___14. AVALON   N. This country wouldn't let Charley in
___15. SALINAS   O. Mr. Steinbeck's home town in California
___16. QUIXOTE   P. It is the great get-together symbol
___17. CANUCKS   Q. The truck
___18. CHILD   R. Author
___19. POLITICS   S. You don't take one, one takes you
___20. TRUTH   T. Sag ___; starting point of the trip
___21. HARRY   U. Kind of sermon in Vermont: ___ & Brimstone
___22. ORLEANS   V. New ___; place where the Cheerleaders demonstrated
___23. REDWOOD   W. Two cans of dog food were left for them
___24. TRIP   X. Fair ___; the boat
___25. ROBBIE   Y. These trees cause wonder & respect in man

Travels With Charley Matching Worksheet 2 Answer Key

Q - 1.	ROCINANTE	A.	Charley was ___ to insecticides
R - 2.	STEINBECK	B.	White Mountains are in this state
B - 3.	MAINE	C.	He wanted to be a hairdresser
L - 4.	ICEBREAKER	D.	____ With Charley
D - 5.	TRAVELS	E.	Topic of family arguments
W - 6.	COYOTES	F.	Lonesome ___; previous occupant of the hotel room
A - 7.	ALLERGIC	G.	Near the end of the book, Mr. Steinbeck gave reasons why he couldn't find the ___ about the country
P - 8.	COFFEE	H.	Maine's migrant farmers
U - 9.	FIRE	I.	Going somewhere with a direction in mind but not caring if you get there or not
T - 10.	HARBOR	J.	Rocinante was named for Don ___'s horse
I - 11.	VACILANDO	K.	The Bad Lands seemed like the work of an evil ____
N - 12.	CANADA	L.	Mr. Steinbeck used Charley as this with strangers
X - 13.	ELEYNE	M.	Deer Isle was like ____
M - 14.	AVALON	N.	This country wouldn't let Charley in
O - 15.	SALINAS	O.	Mr. Steinbeck's home town in California
J - 16.	QUIXOTE	P.	It is the great get-together symbol
H - 17.	CANUCKS	Q.	The truck
K - 18.	CHILD	R.	Author
E - 19.	POLITICS	S.	You don't take one, one takes you
G - 20.	TRUTH	T.	Sag ___; starting point of the trip
F - 21.	HARRY	U.	Kind of sermon in Vermont: ___ & Brimstone
V - 22.	ORLEANS	V.	New ___; place where the Cheerleaders demonstrated
Y - 23.	REDWOOD	W.	Two cans of dog food were left for them
S - 24.	TRIP	X.	Fair ___; the boat
C - 25.	ROBBIE	Y.	These trees cause wonder & respect in man

Travels With Charley Juggle Letters 1

1. AACNAD = 1. _____
   This country wouldn't let Charley in

2. JMEOVA = 2. _____
   Desert Mr. Steinbeck and Charley crossed

3. RLEASTV = 3. _____
   ____ With Charley

4. DHICL = 4. _____
   The Bad Lands seemed like the work of an evil ____

5. ISILPTCO = 5. _____
   Topic of family arguments

6. WEOORDD = 6. _____
   These trees cause wonder & respect in man

7. BEECRAKIER = 7. _____
   Mr. Steinbeck used Charley as this with strangers

8. BREBIO = 8. _____
   He wanted to be a hairdresser

9. LAGISRCE = 9. _____
   Responsible for wiping out most of the redwood trees

10. PIRT =10. _____
    You don't take one, one takes you

11. LIMBEO =11. _____
    These homes were revolutionary

12. RAYHR =12. _____
    Lonesome ___; previous occupant of the hotel room

13. ANATMON =13. _____
    State Mr. Steinbeck considered a great splash of grandeur

14. ABRES =14. _____
    Charley wanted to fight them at Yellowstone

15. UCCASKN =15. _____
    Maine's migrant farmers

16. ELSLD =16. _____
Wisconsin ___; formed by ice during the Ice Age

17. KTEICESBN =17. _____
Author

18. SSRIMIUO =18. _____
This river, according to Mr. Steinbeck, should have been the east-west middle of the country

19. OEXUQIT =19. _____
Rocinante was named for Don ___'s horse

20. WTIN =20. _____
Minneapolis & St. Paul are the ___ Cities

21. NIDM =21. _____
Texas is a state of ____, according to Mr. Steinbeck

22. RLESOAN =22. _____
New ___; place where the Cheerleaders demonstrated

23. ERIF =23. _____
Kind of sermon in Vermont: ___ & Brimstone

Travels With Charley Juggle Letters 1 Answer Key

1. AACNAD = 1. CANADA
This country wouldn't let Charley in

2. JMEOVA = 2. MOJAVE
Desert Mr. Steinbeck and Charley crossed

3. RLEASTV = 3. TRAVELS
____ With Charley

4. DHICL = 4. CHILD
The Bad Lands seemed like the work of an evil ____

5. ISILPTCO = 5. POLITICS
Topic of family arguments

6. WEOORDD = 6. REDWOOD
These trees cause wonder & respect in man

7. BEECRAKIER = 7. ICEBREAKER
Mr. Steinbeck used Charley as this with strangers

8. BREBIO = 8. ROBBIE
He wanted to be a hairdresser

9. LAGISRCE = 9. GLACIERS
Responsible for wiping out most of the redwood trees

10. PIRT = 10. TRIP
You don't take one, one takes you

11. LIMBEO = 11. MOBILE
These homes were revolutionary

12. RAYHR = 12. HARRY
Lonesome ___; previous occupant of the hotel room

13. ANATMON = 13. MONTANA
State Mr. Steinbeck considered a great splash of grandeur

14. ABRES = 14. BEARS
Charley wanted to fight them at Yellowstone

15. UCCASKN = 15. CANUCKS
Maine's migrant farmers

16. ELSLD =16. DELLS
Wisconsin ___; formed by ice during the Ice Age

17. KTEICESBN =17. STEINBECK
Author

18. SSRIMIUO =18. MISSOURI
This river, according to Mr. Steinbeck, should have been the east-west middle of the country

19. OEXUQIT =19. QUIXOTE
Rocinante was named for Don ___'s horse

20. WTIN =20. TWIN
Minneapolis & St. Paul are the ___ Cities

21. NIDM =21. MIND
Texas is a state of ___, according to Mr. Steinbeck

22. RLESOAN =22. ORLEANS
New ___; place where the Cheerleaders demonstrated

23. ERIF =23. FIRE
Kind of sermon in Vermont: ___ & Brimstone

Travels With Charley Juggle Letters 2

1. ORARHB = 1. _____
   Sag ___; starting point of the trip

2. KSREUCTR = 2. _____
   They have their own language, according to Mr. Steinbeck

3. EIWF = 3. _____
   The boat was named for Steinbeck's

4. EYNLEE = 4. _____
   Fair ___; the boat

5. OATINNCER = 5. _____
   The truck

6. FEEOFC = 6. _____
   It is the great get-together symbol

7. REGCLALI = 7. _____
   Charley was ___ to insecticides

8. HAEESEDLERRC = 8. _____
   Group of white women gathered at school to protest desegregation

9. SYETCOO = 9. _____
   Two cans of dog food were left for them

10. SEXAT = 10. _____
    Only state to enter the union by treaty

11. IRIGNIAV = 11. _____
    In this state Mr. Steinbeck realized his trip had ended

12. ACNLADOIV = 12. _____
    Going somewhere with a direction in mind but not caring if you get there or not

13. HTGTUOH = 13. _____
    A man has to have feelings and then words before he can come close to this

14. EINAM = 14. _____
    White Mountains are in this state

15. UTRTH =15. _____

Near the end of the book, Mr. Steinbeck gave reasons why he couldn't find the ___ about the country

16. AOFRG =16. _____

The east-west middle of the country was in ___, ND

17. AVAOLN =17. _____

Deer Isle was like ____

18. AHCOCIG =18. _____

Place where Mr. Steinbeck's wife met him to visit

19. AHLYREC =19. _____

The poodle; companion to Mr. Steinbeck

20. OOTATP =20. _____

Mr. Steinbeck wanted to see these crops in Maine

21. AREBIS =21. _____

Charley didn't have his certificate of vaccination for this

22. ANSILAS =22. _____

Mr. Steinbeck's home town in California

23. AOSDBAASMR =23. _____

Hotel in Chicago: ___ East

Travels With Charley Juggle Letters 2 Answer Key

1. ORARHB = 1. HARBOR
Sag ___; starting point of the trip

2. KSREUCTR = 2. TRUCKERS
They have their own language, according to Mr. Steinbeck

3. EIWF = 3. WIFE
The boat was named for Steinbeck's

4. EYNLEE = 4. ELEYNE
Fair ___; the boat

5. OATINNCER = 5. ROCINANTE
The truck

6. FEEOFC = 6. COFFEE
It is the great get-together symbol

7. REGCLALI = 7. ALLERGIC
Charley was ___ to insecticides

8. HAEESEDLERRC = 8. CHEERLEADERS
Group of white women gathered at school to protest desegregation

9. SYETCOO = 9. COYOTES
Two cans of dog food were left for them

10. SEXAT = 10. TEXAS
Only state to enter the union by treaty

11. IRIGNIAV = 11. VIRGINIA
In this state Mr. Steinbeck realized his trip had ended

12. ACNLADOIV = 12. VACILANDO
Going somewhere with a direction in mind but not caring if you get there or not

13. HTGTUOH = 13. THOUGHT
A man has to have feelings and then words before he can come close to this

14. EINAM = 14. MAINE
White Mountains are in this state

15. UTRTH =15. TRUTH
Near the end of the book, Mr. Steinbeck gave reasons why he couldn't find the ___ about the country

16. AOFRG =16. FARGO
The east-west middle of the country was in ___, ND

17. AVAOLN =17. AVALON
Deer Isle was like ___

18. AHCOCIG =18. CHICAGO
Place where Mr. Steinbeck's wife met him to visit

19. AHLYREC =19. CHARLEY
The poodle; companion to Mr. Steinbeck

20. OOTATP =20. POTATO
Mr. Steinbeck wanted to see these crops in Maine

21. AREBIS =21. RABIES
Charley didn't have his certificate of vaccination for this

22. ANSILAS =22. SALINAS
Mr. Steinbeck's home town in California

23. AOSDBAASMR =23. AMBASSADOR
Hotel in Chicago: ___ East

VOCABULARY RESOURCE MATERIALS

Travels With Charley Vocabulary Word List

No.	Word	Clue/Definition
1.	AESTHETIC	Pertaining to the sense of beauty
2.	ANARCHISM	Theory that all governments are bad & should be abolished
3.	ANTIDOTE	Anything that relieves or counteracts an injurious effect
4.	APEX	Highest point; culmination
5.	APHIDS	Small soft-bodied insects that suck sap from plants
6.	APLOMB	Poise; self-confidence; assurance
7.	ATROPHIED	Wasted away
8.	AVID	Eager
9.	CALLOW	Immature; inexperienced
10.	CLOISTERED	Sheltered
11.	COERCION	Forcing to think or act in a certain manner by threat or force
12.	CONCISE	Expressing much in a few words
13.	CONDUCIVE	Helping to bring about an event
14.	CONSUMMATE	Skilled; perfect
15.	CORPULENCE	Being fat
16.	CORROBORATE	Attested to the truth or accuracy of something
17.	COURTEOUS	Polite
18.	CUR	Inferior or undesirable dog
19.	DAWDLE	Wasting time lingering
20.	DEBRIS	Scattered remains of something broken
21.	DECADENT	Condition or process of moral decay
22.	DEPLORE	Lament; feel or express deep sorrow
23.	DISPEL	To rid of by or as if by driving away or scattering
24.	DOCILE	Teachable; yielding; able to be formed
25.	ELATE	Raise the spirits of; make joyful
26.	ENVOY	Messenger
27.	FRACAS	Noisy quarrel; brawl
28.	GALL	Nerve; impudence
29.	GOADED	Urged; prodded
30.	INALIENABLE	Absolute; not to be given up
31.	INCISED	Cut into
32.	INCORRIGIBLE	Can't be corrected or reformed
33.	INEPT	Clumsy; incompetent
34.	INVECTIVES	Abusive, insulting expressions
35.	KIN	Relatives
36.	LACONIC	Terse; concise; succinct
37.	MEDIOCRE	Neither good or bad; average; ordinary
38.	MISANTHROPY	Hatred of mankind
39.	NUISANCE	A source of inconvenience or bother
40.	OBLIQUE	Indirect or evasive in meaning or expression; not straightforward
41.	OBSEQUIOUS	Full of servile compliance; fawning
42.	OBSOLESCENCE	Being replaced by something newer
43.	OGRE	Anyone especially cruel, brutish, or hideous
44.	ORGY	A revel involving unrestrained indulgence
45.	OSTENTATION	Showiness to impress others
46.	PANDEMONIUM	Uproar & noise
47.	PARADOX	Seemingly contradictory statement that may nonetheless be true

Travels With Charley Vocabulary Word List Continued

No. Word	Clue/Definition
48. PERIPATETIC	Roaming; wandering
49. PERNICIOUS	Destructive; harmful
50. PISCINE	Relating to fish
51. POSTULATE	Statement generally accepted without proof
52. PRECIOUS	Valuable
53. PREMISE	Statement on which an argument is based or from which a conclusion is drawn
54. QUALMS	Bad or uneasy feeling
55. SEMANTIC	Relating to language
56. SIEGE	Attack
57. SUBTLETIES	Details; refinements
58. TACITURN	Not talkative
59. TAWDRY	Gaudy & cheap
60. TRAVAIL	Labor
61. UBIQUITOUS	Seeming to be everywhere at one time
62. VAGUELY	Not clearly expressed or defined
63. VICARIOUS	Experienced through imaginative participation in the experiences of others
64. VINTAGE	Classic; characterized by enduring appeal
65. VITALITY	Energy; liveliness
66. WREST	To obtain forcefully
67. ZENITH	Upper region of the sky

Travels With Charley Vocabulary Word Search

```
T I N C O R R I G I B L E B M O L P A
A A W U H G C G W D I A V Z E R Z I S
T V W Z I L R C B A E C M V D G C S V
R Y V D A S P E V V L O I K I Y V C S
O H P P R K A A D I A N F D O I D I B
P N E O V Y R N H D T I O T C C R N B
H X R S A T A S C A E C Z A R B W E T
I Z N T G D D I G E I S R C E G A L L
E Y I U U K O E H L U I I D V N Y B H
D X C L E T X G E O O T D W O L L A C
J V I A L C P E I U E S I C N O C N L
I S O T Y D R C S T D T S E R W N E O
N E U E S D E D A O G N A W U Y O I I
C M S S N R M P H J E E C M T D I L S
I A Y D P H I G L L Y D A Z I B C A T
S N F I Z R S B D O M A R X C F R N E
E T E H E S E W V C R C F C A Q E I R
D I S P E L A N I K Z E N I T H O U E
B C H A T D E A N T I D O T E W C Q D
```

ANTIDOTE	CUR	GALL	OGRE	SIEGE
APEX	DAWDLE	GOADED	ORGY	TACITURN
APHIDS	DEBRIS	INALIENABLE	PARADOX	TAWDRY
APLOMB	DECADENT	INCISED	PERIPATETIC	TRAVAIL
ATROPHIED	DEPLORE	INCORRIGIBLE	PERNICIOUS	VAGUELY
AVID	DISPEL	INEPT	PISCINE	VICARIOUS
CALLOW	DOCILE	KIN	POSTULATE	VINTAGE
CLOISTERED	ELATE	LACONIC	PRECIOUS	WREST
COERCION	ENVOY	MEDIOCRE	PREMISE	ZENITH
CONCISE	FRACAS	NUISANCE	SEMANTIC	

Travels With Charley Vocabulary Word Search Answer Key

[Word search grid]

ANTIDOTE	CUR	GALL	OGRE	SIEGE
APEX	DAWDLE	GOADED	ORGY	TACITURN
APHIDS	DEBRIS	INALIENABLE	PARADOX	TAWDRY
APLOMB	DECADENT	INCISED	PERIPATETIC	TRAVAIL
ATROPHIED	DEPLORE	INCORRIGIBLE	PERNICIOUS	VAGUELY
AVID	DISPEL	INEPT	PISCINE	VICARIOUS
CALLOW	DOCILE	KIN	POSTULATE	VINTAGE
CLOISTERED	ELATE	LACONIC	PRECIOUS	WREST
COERCION	ENVOY	MEDIOCRE	PREMISE	ZENITH
CONCISE	FRACAS	NUISANCE	SEMANTIC	

Travels With Charley Vocabulary Crossword

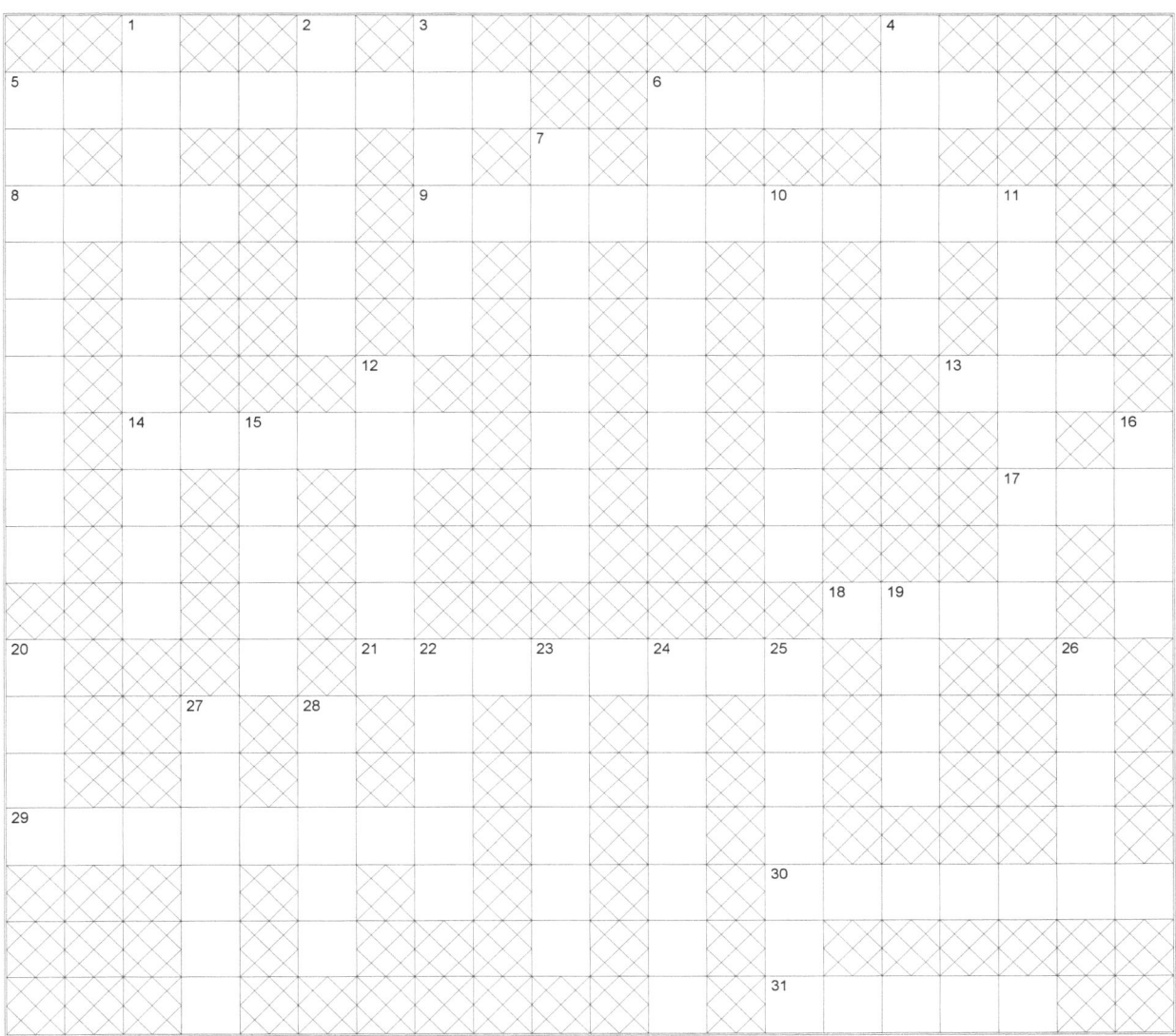

Across
5. Pertaining to the sense of beauty
6. Immature; inexperienced
8. Highest point; culmination
9. Uproar & noise
13. Relatives
14. Gaudy & cheap
17. Inferior or undesirable dog
18. Anyone especially cruel, brutish, or hideous
21. Relating to language
29. Condition or process of moral decay
30. Cut into
31. Messenger

Down
1. Showiness to impress others
2. Scattered remains of something broken
3. To rid of by or as if by driving away or scattering
4. Teachable; yielding; able to be formed
5. Theory that all governments are bad & should be abolished
6. Forcing to think or act in a certain manner by threat or force
7. Anything that relieves or counteracts an injurious effect
10. Indirect or evasive in meaning or expression; not straightforward
11. Neither good or bad; average; ordinary
12. Noisy quarrel; brawl
15. To obtain forcefully
16. A revel involving unrestrained indulgence
19. Nerve; impudence
20. Eager
22. Raise the spirits of; make joyful
23. Small soft-bodied insects that suck sap from plants
24. Labor
25. Expressing much in a few words
26. Attack
27. Urged; prodded
28. Clumsy; incompetent

Travels With Charley Vocabulary Crossword Answer Key

Across
- 5. Pertaining to the sense of beauty
- 6. Immature; inexperienced
- 8. Highest point; culmination
- 9. Uproar & noise
- 13. Relatives
- 14. Gaudy & cheap
- 17. Inferior or undesirable dog
- 18. Anyone especially cruel, brutish, or hideous
- 21. Relating to language
- 29. Condition or process of moral decay
- 30. Cut into
- 31. Messenger

Down
- 1. Showiness to impress others
- 2. Scattered remains of something broken
- 3. To rid of by or as if by driving away or scattering
- 4. Teachable; yielding; able to be formed
- 5. Theory that all governments are bad & should be abolished
- 6. Forcing to think or act in a certain manner by threat or force
- 7. Anything that relieves or counteracts an injurious effect
- 10. Indirect or evasive in meaning or expression; not straightforward
- 11. Neither good or bad; average; ordinary
- 12. Noisy quarrel; brawl
- 15. To obtain forcefully
- 16. A revel involving unrestrained indulgence
- 19. Nerve; impudence
- 20. Eager
- 22. Raise the spirits of; make joyful
- 23. Small soft-bodied insects that suck sap from plants
- 24. Labor
- 25. Expressing much in a few words
- 26. Attack
- 27. Urged; prodded
- 28. Clumsy; incompetent

Travels With Charley Vocabulary Matching 1

___ 1. CUR A. Classic; characterized by enduring appeal
___ 2. SUBTLETIES B. Anyone especially cruel, brutish, or hideous
___ 3. AVID C. Inferior or undesirable dog
___ 4. COERCION D. Wasting time lingering
___ 5. AESTHETIC E. Relating to language
___ 6. DECADENT F. Condition or process of moral decay
___ 7. POSTULATE G. Noisy quarrel; brawl
___ 8. DAWDLE H. Roaming; wandering
___ 9. SEMANTIC I. Forcing to think or act in a certain manner by threat or force
___ 10. ANTIDOTE J. Eager
___ 11. PERIPATETIC K. Seemingly contradictory statement that may nonetheless be true
___ 12. PARADOX L. Labor
___ 13. VITALITY M. Anything that relieves or counteracts an injurious effect
___ 14. GALL N. Statement generally accepted without proof
___ 15. TRAVAIL O. Energy; liveliness
___ 16. VINTAGE P. Pertaining to the sense of beauty
___ 17. FRACAS Q. Not talkative
___ 18. TAWDRY R. Experienced through imaginative participation in the experiences of others
___ 19. OGRE S. Gaudy & cheap
___ 20. PISCINE T. Destructive; harmful
___ 21. TACITURN U. Upper region of the sky
___ 22. VICARIOUS V. Nerve; impudence
___ 23. ANARCHISM W. Relating to fish
___ 24. ZENITH X. Theory that all governments are bad & should be abolished
___ 25. PERNICIOUS Y. Details; refinements

Travels With Charley Vocabulary Matching 1 Answer Key

C - 1. CUR	A.	Classic; characterized by enduring appeal
Y - 2. SUBTLETIES	B.	Anyone especially cruel, brutish, or hideous
J - 3. AVID	C.	Inferior or undesirable dog
I - 4. COERCION	D.	Wasting time lingering
P - 5. AESTHETIC	E.	Relating to language
F - 6. DECADENT	F.	Condition or process of moral decay
N - 7. POSTULATE	G.	Noisy quarrel; brawl
D - 8. DAWDLE	H.	Roaming; wandering
E - 9. SEMANTIC	I.	Forcing to think or act in a certain manner by threat or force
M - 10. ANTIDOTE	J.	Eager
H - 11. PERIPATETIC	K.	Seemingly contradictory statement that may nonetheless be true
K - 12. PARADOX	L.	Labor
O - 13. VITALITY	M.	Anything that relieves or counteracts an injurious effect
V - 14. GALL	N.	Statement generally accepted without proof
L - 15. TRAVAIL	O.	Energy; liveliness
A - 16. VINTAGE	P.	Pertaining to the sense of beauty
G - 17. FRACAS	Q.	Not talkative
S - 18. TAWDRY	R.	Experienced through imaginative participation in the experiences of others
B - 19. OGRE	S.	Gaudy & cheap
W - 20. PISCINE	T.	Destructive; harmful
Q - 21. TACITURN	U.	Upper region of the sky
R - 22. VICARIOUS	V.	Nerve; impudence
X - 23. ANARCHISM	W.	Relating to fish
U - 24. ZENITH	X.	Theory that all governments are bad & should be abolished
T - 25. PERNICIOUS	Y.	Details; refinements

Travels With Charley Vocabulay Matching 2

___ 1. CORROBORATE   A. Immature; inexperienced
___ 2. SUBTLETIES   B. Valuable
___ 3. GOADED   C. Small soft-bodied insects that suck sap from plants
___ 4. CONDUCIVE   D. To obtain forcefully
___ 5. APHIDS   E. Urged; prodded
___ 6. FRACAS   F. Details; refinements
___ 7. MEDIOCRE   G. Helping to bring about an event
___ 8. WREST   H. Relating to language
___ 9. PRECIOUS   I. Attested to the truth or accuracy of something
___10. OSTENTATION   J. Neither good or bad; average; ordinary
___11. TRAVAIL   K. Relating to fish
___12. INVECTIVES   L. Destructive; harmful
___13. GALL   M. Noisy quarrel; brawl
___14. VAGUELY   N. Classic; characterized by enduring appeal
___15. VINTAGE   O. Nerve; impudence
___16. ELATE   P. Theory that all governments are bad & should be abolished
___17. PERNICIOUS   Q. Not clearly expressed or defined
___18. CALLOW   R. Raise the spirits of; make joyful
___19. VITALITY   S. Showiness to impress others
___20. ANARCHISM   T. Energy; liveliness
___21. OBLIQUE   U. Expressing much in a few words
___22. DOCILE   V. Labor
___23. SEMANTIC   W. Indirect or evasive in meaning or expression; not straightforward
___24. PISCINE   X. Abusive, insulting expressions
___25. CONCISE   Y. Teachable; yielding; able to be formed

Travels With Charley Vocabulary Matching 2 Answer Key

I - 1.	CORROBORATE	A. Immature; inexperienced
F - 2.	SUBTLETIES	B. Valuable
E - 3.	GOADED	C. Small soft-bodied insects that suck sap from plants
G - 4.	CONDUCIVE	D. To obtain forcefully
C - 5.	APHIDS	E. Urged; prodded
M - 6.	FRACAS	F. Details; refinements
J - 7.	MEDIOCRE	G. Helping to bring about an event
D - 8.	WREST	H. Relating to language
B - 9.	PRECIOUS	I. Attested to the truth or accuracy of something
S - 10.	OSTENTATION	J. Neither good or bad; average; ordinary
V - 11.	TRAVAIL	K. Relating to fish
X - 12.	INVECTIVES	L. Destructive; harmful
O - 13.	GALL	M. Noisy quarrel; brawl
Q - 14.	VAGUELY	N. Classic; characterized by enduring appeal
N - 15.	VINTAGE	O. Nerve; impudence
R - 16.	ELATE	P. Theory that all governments are bad & should be abolished
L - 17.	PERNICIOUS	Q. Not clearly expressed or defined
A - 18.	CALLOW	R. Raise the spirits of; make joyful
T - 19.	VITALITY	S. Showiness to impress others
P - 20.	ANARCHISM	T. Energy; liveliness
W - 21.	OBLIQUE	U. Expressing much in a few words
Y - 22.	DOCILE	V. Labor
H - 23.	SEMANTIC	W. Indirect or evasive in meaning or expression; not straightforward
K - 24.	PISCINE	X. Abusive, insulting expressions
U - 25.	CONCISE	Y. Teachable; yielding; able to be formed

Travels With Charley Vocabulary Juggle Letters 1

1. HSIADP = 1. _____
   Small soft-bodied insects that suck sap from plants

2. ROCSAIUIV = 2. _____
   Experienced through imaginative participation in the experiences of others

3. DCNECUVOI = 3. _____
   Helping to bring about an event

4. RISBED = 4. _____
   Scattered remains of something broken

5. PETIIPCRAET = 5. _____
   Roaming; wandering

6. TLEAE = 6. _____
   Raise the spirits of; make joyful

7. EEMRISP = 7. _____
   Statement on which an argument is based or from which a conclusion is drawn

8. LGEUAVY = 8. _____
   Not clearly expressed or defined

9. BUOEQLI = 9. _____
   Indirect or evasive in meaning or expression; not straightforward

10. RNSCUIPEOI = 10. _____
    Destructive; harmful

11. ENITP = 11. _____
    Clumsy; incompetent

12. ICEIPNS = 12. _____
    Relating to fish

13. GLAL = 13. _____
    Nerve; impudence

14. RIOECMDE = 14. _____
    Neither good or bad; average; ordinary

15. SIDPLE =15. _____
To rid of by or as if by driving away or scattering

16. ILNCOAC =16. _____
Terse; concise; succinct

17. EGRO =17. _____
Anyone especially cruel, brutish, or hideous

18. NCSSEBCLOOEE =18. _____
Being replaced by something newer

19. ROCCONIE =19. _____
Forcing to think or act in a certain manner by threat or force

20. PECCLEURON =20. _____
Being fat

21. OESNCCI =21. _____
Expressing much in a few words

22. AERRROBOCTO =22. _____
Attested to the truth or accuracy of something

23. PEODLRE =23. _____
Lament; feel or express deep sorrow

24. EVOYN =24. _____
Messenger

25. QLUAMS =25. _____
Bad or uneasy feeling

26. UREUSOTOC =26. _____
Polite

27. DAGDEO =27. _____
Urged; prodded

28. EHDOPIRTA =28. _____
Wasted away

29. NIEDCSI =29. _____
Cut into

30. OBPMLA =30. _____
Poise; self-confidence; assurance

31. EISGE =31. _____
Attack

32. NAMUCTOMSE =32. _____
Skilled; perfect

33. AUITCTNR =33. _____
Not talkative

34. VRTLAIA =34. _____
Labor

Travels With Charley Vocabulary Juggle Letters 1 Answer Key

1. HSIADP = 1. APHIDS
Small soft-bodied insects that suck sap from plants

2. ROCSAIUIV = 2. VICARIOUS
Experienced through imaginative participation in the experiences of others

3. DCNECUVOI = 3. CONDUCIVE
Helping to bring about an event

4. RISBED = 4. DEBRIS
Scattered remains of something broken

5. PETIIPCRAET = 5. PERIPATETIC
Roaming; wandering

6. TLEAE = 6. ELATE
Raise the spirits of; make joyful

7. EEMRISP = 7. PREMISE
Statement on which an argument is based or from which a conclusion is drawn

8. LGEUAVY = 8. VAGUELY
Not clearly expressed or defined

9. BUOEQLI = 9. OBLIQUE
Indirect or evasive in meaning or expression; not straightforward

10. RNSCUIPEOI = 10. PERNICIOUS
Destructive; harmful

11. ENITP = 11. INEPT
Clumsy; incompetent

12. ICEIPNS = 12. PISCINE
Relating to fish

13. GLAL = 13. GALL
Nerve; impudence

14. RIOECMDE = 14. MEDIOCRE
Neither good or bad; average; ordinary

15. SIDPLE =15. DISPEL
To rid of by or as if by driving away or scattering

16. ILNCOAC =16. LACONIC
Terse; concise; succinct

17. EGRO =17. OGRE
Anyone especially cruel, brutish, or hideous

18. NCSSEBCLOOEE =18. OBSOLESCENCE
Being replaced by something newer

19. ROCCONIE =19. COERCION
Forcing to think or act in a certain manner by threat or force

20. PECCLEURON =20. CORPULENCE
Being fat

21. OESNCCI =21. CONCISE
Expressing much in a few words

22. AERRROBOCTO =22. CORROBORATE
Attested to the truth or accuracy of something

23. PEODLRE =23. DEPLORE
Lament; feel or express deep sorrow

24. EVOYN =24. ENVOY
Messenger

25. QLUAMS =25. QUALMS
Bad or uneasy feeling

26. UREUSOTOC =26. COURTEOUS
Polite

27. DAGDEO =27. GOADED
Urged; prodded

28. EHDOPIRTA =28. ATROPHIED
Wasted away

29. NIEDCSI =29. INCISED
Cut into

30. OBPMLA =30. APLOMB
Poise; self-confidence; assurance

31. EISGE =31. SIEGE
Attack

32. NAMUCTOMSE =32. CONSUMMATE
Skilled; perfect

33. AUITCTNR =33. TACITURN
Not talkative

34. VRTLAIA =34. TRAVAIL
Labor

Travels With Charley Vocabulary Juggle Letters 2

1. SWTER = 1. _____
   To obtain forcefully

2. ACTSIMEN = 2. _____
   Relating to language

3. WLCOLA = 3. _____
   Immature; inexperienced

4. PUATLSOET = 4. _____
   Statement generally accepted without proof

5. TCESILDERO = 5. _____
   Sheltered

6. IHACSRNAM = 6. _____
   Theory that all governments are bad & should be abolished

7. RRCNIOILEBIG = 7. _____
   Can't be corrected or reformed

8. CSINNEAU = 8. _____
   A source of inconvenience or bother

9. CSARFA = 9. _____
   Noisy quarrel; brawl

10. CSUOEPRI =10. _____
    Valuable

11. NPMODUMAIEN =11. _____
    Uproar & noise

12. YTWARD =12. _____
    Gaudy & cheap

13. MONRYAISHTP =13. _____
    Hatred of mankind

14. NIZETH =14. _____
    Upper region of the sky

15. XPAE =15. _____
    Highest point; culmination

16. ISUUBUITQO =16. _____
Seeming to be everywhere at one time

17. DVIA =17. _____
Eager

18. LWDEAD =18. _____
Wasting time lingering

19. OLIECD =19. _____
Teachable; yielding; able to be formed

20. AXROPAD =20. _____
Seemingly contradictory statement that may nonetheless be true

21. RGYO =21. _____
A revel involving unrestrained indulgence

22. TESEVCVIIN =22. _____
Abusive, insulting expressions

23. NIK =23. _____
Relatives

24. RCU =24. _____
Inferior or undesirable dog

25. TTVYIAIL =25. _____
Energy; liveliness

26. EVGTNAI =26. _____
Classic; characterized by enduring appeal

27. QEBSOUUOSI =27. _____
Full of servile compliance; fawning

29. TNTSEITOAON =29. _____
Showiness to impress others

28. ELEBTUSITS =28. _____
Details; refinements

29. IODTATNE =29. _____
Anything that relieves or counteracts an injurious effect

30. EDTNAEDC =30. _____
Condition or process of moral decay

164

Travels With Charley Vocabulary Juggle Letters 2 Answer Key

1. SWTER = 1. WREST
   To obtain forcefully

2. ACTSIMEN = 2. SEMANTIC
   Relating to language

3. WLCOLA = 3. CALLOW
   Immature; inexperienced

4. PUATLSOET = 4. POSTULATE
   Statement generally accepted without proof

5. TCESILDERO = 5. CLOISTERED
   Sheltered

6. IHACSRNAM = 6. ANARCHISM
   Theory that all governments are bad & should be abolished

7. RRCNIOILEBIG = 7. INCORRIGIBLE
   Can't be corrected or reformed

8. CSINNEAU = 8. NUISANCE
   A source of inconvenience or bother

9. CSARFA = 9. FRACAS
   Noisy quarrel; brawl

10. CSUOEPRI = 10. PRECIOUS
    Valuable

11. NPMODUMAIEN = 11. PANDEMONIUM
    Uproar & noise

12. YTWARD = 12. TAWDRY
    Gaudy & cheap

13. MONRYAISHTP = 13. MISANTHROPY
    Hatred of mankind

14. NIZETH = 14. ZENITH
    Upper region of the sky

15. XPAE = 15. APEX
    Highest point; culmination

16. ISUUBUITQO = 16. UBIQUITOUS
Seeming to be everywhere at one time

17. DVIA = 17. AVID
Eager

18. LWDEAD = 18. DAWDLE
Wasting time lingering

19. OLIECD = 19. DOCILE
Teachable; yielding; able to be formed

20. AXROPAD = 20. PARADOX
Seemingly contradictory statement that may nonetheless be true

21. RGYO = 21. ORGY
A revel involving unrestrained indulgence

22. TESEVCVIIN = 22. INVECTIVES
Abusive, insulting expressions

23. NIK = 23. KIN
Relatives

24. RCU = 24. CUR
Inferior or undesirable dog

25. TTVYIAIL = 25. VITALITY
Energy; liveliness

26. EVGTNAI = 26. VINTAGE
Classic; characterized by enduring appeal

27. QEBSOUUOSI = 27. OBSEQUIOUS
Full of servile compliance; fawning

28. TNTSEITOAON = 28. OSTENTATION
Showiness to impress others

29. ELEBTUSITS = 29. SUBTLETIES
Details; refinements

30. IODTATNE = 30. ANTIDOTE
Anything that relieves or counteracts an injurious effect

31. EDTNAEDC = 31. DECADENT
Condition or process of moral decay

32. ISHTETAEC = 32. AESTHETIC
Pertaining to the sense of beauty

www.ingramcontent.com/pod-product-compliance
Lightning Source LLC
LaVergne TN
LVHW081534060526
838200LV00048B/2086